# OTHER BOOKS BY PEG KEHRET

*Ghost Dog Secrets*

*Runaway Twin*

*Stolen Children*

*Trapped*

*Abduction*

*Spy Cat*

*The Stranger Next Door*

*Don't Tell Anyone*

*I'm Not Who You Think I Am*

*Searching for Candlestick Park*

*Earthquake Terror*

*Danger at the Fair*

*The Richest Kids in Town*

*Night of Fear*

*Horror at the Haunted House*

*Terror at the Zoo*

*Sisters Long Ago*

*Cages*

*Nightmare Mountain*

Animals
Welcome

# PEG KEHRET

# Animals Welcome

*A Life of Reading, Writing, and Rescue*

DUTTON CHILDREN'S BOOKS

*An imprint of Penguin Group (USA) Inc.*

DUTTON CHILDREN'S BOOKS
*A division of Penguin Young Readers Group*

PUBLISHED BY THE PENGUIN GROUP

Penguin Group (USA) Inc., 375 Hudson Street, New York, New York 10014, U.S.A. | Penguin Group (Canada), 90 Eglinton Avenue East, Suite 700, Toronto, Ontario, Canada M4P 2Y3 (a division of Pearson Penguin Canada Inc.) | Penguin Books Ltd, 80 Strand, London WC2R 0RL, England | Penguin Ireland, 25 St Stephen's Green, Dublin 2, Ireland (a division of Penguin Books Ltd) | Penguin Group (Australia), 250 Camberwell Road, Camberwell, Victoria 3124, Australia (a division of Pearson Australia Group Pty Ltd) | Penguin Books India Pvt Ltd, 11 Community Centre, Panchsheel Park, New Delhi - 110 017, India | Penguin Group (NZ), 67 Apollo Drive, Rosedale, Auckland 0632, New Zealand (a division of Pearson New Zealand Ltd) | Penguin Books (South Africa) (Pty) Ltd, 24 Sturdee Avenue, Rosebank, Johannesburg 2196, South Africa | Penguin Books Ltd, Registered Offices: 80 Strand, London WC2R 0RL, England

CIP Data is available.

Published in the United States by Dutton Children's Books,
a division of Penguin Young Readers Group
345 Hudson Street, New York, New York 10014
www.penguin.com/youngreaders

Designed by Irene Vandervoort

Printed in USA     First Edition

10 9 8 7 6 5 4 3 2 1

ISBN 978-0-525-42399-7

*For Anne, Kevin, Brett, and Eric Konen,*
*who share my love for the cabin and its critters*

*and in loving memory of Carl*

# CONTENTS

*Introduction*                                          *xi*

1. *Two Tuxedos*                                        *3*

2. *I Didn't Want His Owner to Find Him*                *16*

3. *The Cats Who Had Been Shot*                         *27*

4. *Sad Farewells*                                      *41*

5. *The Pet I've Never Petted*                          *52*

6. *Living with Wildlife*                               *63*

7. *My Life Changed Forever*                            *83*

8. *I Bailed Him Out, and Then He Bit Me*               *99*

9. *Short Stays*                                        *111*

10. *The Poacher*                                       *122*

11. *Throwaway Cat*                                     *134*

12. *Breaking My Own Rule*                              *144*

13. *Many Surprises*                                    *160*

14. *I Wonder What's Next?*                             *171*

Animals
Welcome

# Introduction

Most of my books include an animal. I've written about elephants, bears, llamas, dogs, cats, chimpanzees, a rabbit, a pig, a 'possum, a horse, a pony, and a monkey. I volunteer for animal welfare groups, and part of my royalties go to support a spay/neuter clinic that offers inexpensive surgeries to low-income pet owners.

I'm always thrilled when I glimpse deer or other wild animals in their natural habitat. My fondness for farm animals, especially pigs, cows, and sheep, is the reason I'm a vegetarian. I've also helped rescue and care for dozens of domestic animals.

I began to observe and learn about forest animals when I moved to my dream house, a log cabin on ten wooded acres adjoining hundreds more acres of forest land in Washington State. The first time my husband, Carl, and I walked this property, we saw deer grazing in the woods. Instead of traffic noise, we heard birdsong. What a great place to write my books, and for Carl to conduct his business of restoring antique musical instruments.

*A view from my back porch*

Over the years, we had lived in more than one city but we both preferred country living. Eighteen years earlier, we had restored an old country farmhouse, only to have the suburbs gradually creep out and surround us. When we could walk from the farmhouse to McDonald's, we knew it was time to move.

The land where we built the cabin, with its acres of trees and native wildlife, seemed so far removed from fast-food restaurants, gas stations, and crowded shops that it felt almost as if we were in a different state. Having animals roam the property made me appreciate it even more.

I've always loved animals. When I was a child, we had a family dog—first Skippy, when I was little, and then B.J. In high school, I had an ongoing argument with two of my classmates, twin boys who insisted cats were the best pets, while I argued that dogs were superior. Now I know we were both correct: dogs are wonderful animals and so are cats.

Carl grew up on a dairy farm. While his family cared for many animals, they had no house pets. Even so, he shared my instinctive tenderness for the critters. Soon after we were married, we adopted a kitten, and from that day on at least one animal always shared our home.

When we moved to the cabin, we stood at the windows and watched deer, elk, 'possums, and rabbits. We rejoiced to see them and vowed to protect them.

We studied the best ways to help the wildlife, who so often get chased away when humans enter their territory, and realized that befriending the animals meant keeping their habitat healthy. First we had our land certified as a wildlife sanctuary. Next we enrolled in a state reforestation program where we took classes in how to care for our woods. Pledging to replace downed trees and to be good stewards of the land, we left all of the property except the house site and driveway, which fire regulations required that we keep a certain size, in its natural state.

Brush piles became shelter for rabbits and other small creatures, and when we fenced the property to keep our dog in, we followed the deer paths to the property lines and built the fences low enough in those places so that even fawns could come and go with ease.

Carl created a nature trail that winds through the woods. Blacktail deer quickly discovered the nature trail and made it part of their daily travel. I was living in Paradise. I still am.

Shortly after we moved to the cabin, our oldest granddaughter, Brett, came to spend the day. She was nine at the time. After she left, I found a message scrawled in the dirt under my office window: ANIMALS WELCOME. Apparently, the critters can read, because I've had four-legged visitors ever since.

Since we had watched for deer during her visit, I'm quite sure that Brett intended her message for the forest animals. They came, in abundance, in the years ahead, but so did domestic animals in need of help, a development I had not anticipated.

This book is about some of those animals—the ones who live in the forest, the rescued ones I brought to the cabin, and those in need who found me on their own, beginning with Buddy, the tuxedo cat who moved to my woods around the same time I did.

## Two Tuxedos

When Carl and I moved to the cabin, we had two cats—Pete, a Siamese mix adopted from an animal shelter, and Molly, a tabby whom we rescued in Indiana when I was doing school visits there. We let them go out during the day in nice weather, if they wanted to, but we always called them home when it started to get dark and kept them indoors at night. As an incentive to come when we called, they got their favorite moist food, referred to as kitty-num-num, only at that time.

We walked daily on the nature trail or around the rest of the property with our cairn terrier, Daisy, who came from the same shelter as Pete, in the lead. Pete and Molly usually followed us, making it quite a parade. We had lived here only a short time when, on one of our evening walks, I glanced over my shoulder to be sure Pete and Molly were still with us, and saw a big tuxedo cat—black with a white chest and white paws—bringing up the rear!

"We've added a cat," I told Carl.

He looked back. "I wonder where he came from."

Daisy, who loved all creatures of any size or species, looked, too. Then she wagged her tail and continued on our walk.

To our surprise, Pete and Molly accepted this newcomer as if they already knew him, and we wondered if they had become acquainted when they were outdoors without us.

The new cat followed us on the entire loop of the trail, then sat on the porch with us to watch the sunset. He even jumped in Carl's lap. When we went inside, taking Pete and Molly with us, the tuxedo cat peered wistfully through the glass door, watching us.

I called my closest neighbors, to ask if the cat might belong to them. "Oh, that's Buddy," my neighbor said. "He isn't ours, but he hangs out around here sometimes. We feed him once in a while."

Once in a while? Buddy must be a good mouser, because he appeared to be well fed.

Within a week, Buddy had made it clear that he'd switched

his allegiance from the neighbors to us. Each morning when we got up, he was waiting on the porch. If I went outside, he hurried to rub against my legs, and he accompanied us on every walk, even if Pete and Molly chose not to come. More than once, I spotted all three cats sitting together in the sun. At night, Buddy watched forlornly from the porch as Pete and Molly came inside.

*Pete and Molly*

I put food and water on the porch for him, but I still felt sorry for Buddy, left outside every night while his two cat friends came indoors.

"Three cats wouldn't be that much more trouble than two," I said.

"He already gets along with Pete and Molly," Carl said.

We took Buddy to the vet and had him neutered. He got all his vaccinations; he got wormed. When we picked him up that afternoon, we put a collar and an ID tag on him. Then we took him home and carried him inside.

*Buddy*

The trouble began immediately. The cats, who had gotten along splendidly when they were all outdoors together, were suddenly mortal enemies when they occupied the same house. Pete and Molly hissed and growled and acted as if we'd been invaded by aliens. Buddy seemed determined to show them who was boss. Fur flew as Buddy and Pete fought. Molly jumped into the fray, biting and scratching.

We quickly separated Buddy from the other two, and kept them apart overnight. Then we reintroduced him slowly, the way we would if we had brought home a new cat that they'd never seen before. We put Pete and Molly in the room where Buddy had spent the night, and let Buddy have the rest of the house. After a few hours, we switched. The next day, we let them see each other.

Finally we let Buddy be in the same room with one cat at a time. Pete went first. Both cats growled, circling each other with their ears flat, as if they expected me to say, "Go!" so the fight could start. Molly wasn't any better. When it was her turn with Buddy, her fur looked like she'd been plugged in to an electrical outlet. She hissed; Buddy took a swipe at her.

Nothing helped. The fighting continued, and expanded to fights outdoors as well as in. If we wanted to get any sleep, we had to keep them separated at night. Remembering how well they got along initially, we tried to be patient.

I discovered a terrible abscess on Pete's neck, where Buddy had bitten or scratched him. The vet lanced it and sterilized the area. A week later, we rushed Buddy to the vet with a high fever. It turned out he had an abscess, too.

Molly, who was much smaller than the two male cats, began spending a lot of time hiding under the bed. Daisy got upset, too, whenever a catfight broke out. I had to stay constantly vigilant to try to prevent trouble.

"This is not working," Carl said.

I agreed. We decided that it would be best to find someone who wanted to adopt Buddy.

Luckily, some retired friends, Ginny and Bob, offered to take him. They were at home most of the time and had no other animals. Their only concern was that they didn't know how to clip a cat's toenails, so I promised that Buddy's adoption included having me come to clip his toenails for the rest of his life.

Buddy moved in with our friends the next day. We gave them his bed, a scratching post, and his favorite toys. They claimed they got the bargain of the decade, but I knew we were the fortunate ones. Much as I liked Buddy, I felt a huge relief when we went home without him.

Ginny and Bob adored Buddy, and he thrived as the only animal in the house. As promised, I went to visit every couple of months, taking the toenail clippers with me. We called it Buddy's Spa Day.

Buddy became an indoor cat and never once tried to sneak out. Why would he? He had gone from being a needy stray, peering in the window at more fortunate cats, to being a pampered pet himself.

We never figured out why Pete and Molly were so friendly to Buddy when they were all outdoors, and so aggressive when he came inside. If they were protecting their territory, why hadn't they attacked Buddy when he first arrived? And why did Buddy change from a mild-mannered cat to a mean fighter after he got what we thought he wanted?

Later, when I began to write the Pete the Cat books, I dedicated *The Stranger Next Door* to the friends who adopted Buddy.

Not long after Buddy's successful adoption, we flew to Minnesota to attend the funeral of Carl's stepfather. Carl's mother had married Herman a few years after Carl's dad died. Herman had never had a pet. He grew up on a farm, where animals were kept outdoors, and had been a farmer himself until he retired. He was a bachelor until he married Carl's mother. She had multiple allergies that prevented her from having animals indoors.

When they visited us, Herman always enjoyed our cats. Once, when we took him and Carl's mom to visit the animal shelter where we volunteered, Herman saw a gray cat awaiting adoption and was distressed because they couldn't take it. Years later, he still mentioned that gray cat and hoped it had found a good home.

After Carl's mother died, Herman lived alone until a friend offered him a five-year-old cat. Chester was a big black-and-white tuxedo cat, the same as Buddy had been, and Herman doted on that cat for the rest of his life.

Herman died suddenly, of a heart attack, and when we arrived two days later, we asked the family members who lived nearby what had happened to Chester.

"I guess he's still at Herman's house," we were told.

We hurried to the house, where we found a forlorn Chester, meowing and looking for his friend. I cleaned out his litter box while Carl washed his bowls and gave him fresh water and food. Later that day, the whole family gathered to discuss the distribution of Herman's household goods. We asked, "Has anyone made arrangements for Chester? Who's going to take him?"

"We can take him to the dog pound," someone said. "They accept cats, too."

My eyes met Carl's, and I could tell he was as shocked as I was by that suggestion.

"We can't take Chester to the pound," I said. "He was Herman's beloved companion. We need to provide for him, to see that he has a good home."

We started asking the relatives who lived in that area if anyone wanted to take Chester. One of Carl's nephews said Chester could come to his house—but he and his wife had three young children, two big dogs, and two outdoor cats. Chester was used to a quiet indoor life with an elderly man; I was sure he'd be terrified and miserable if he suddenly found himself in the midst of all that commotion.

Someone else said Chester could be a barn cat on his farm. I nixed that idea, too. I know the offer was well intended and no doubt I sounded way too fussy, but I could not do that to mild old Chester. The barn mice probably would have chased him!

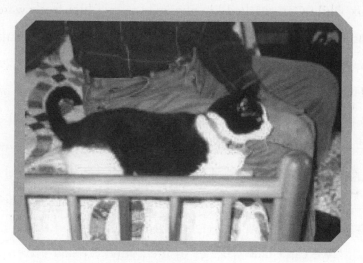

*Chester*

We had arrived the day before the funeral and had plane tickets back home for the day after. We had no time to try to find a proper home for a cat.

"We'll have to take him with us," I said.

Carl nodded agreement.

I called our airline and learned that we'd be charged a seventy-five-dollar pet travel fee. Chester had to have a certificate showing he was healthy and had been vaccinated within the last three months, and he had to be in a carrier that fit under the seat. Chester was current on his vaccines, but it had been longer than three months since he got them, so the morning of the funeral, we took him to a veterinarian to be examined and revaccinated. Then we found a pet store and purchased an airline-approved carrier. The next morning, before we left for the airport, we picked up Chester and the three of us headed home.

The vet had given us a tranquilizer, in case Chester got too nervous about traveling, but we never had to give it to him. He was an angel, not making a sound the whole time. About halfway through the flight, I put the carrier on my lap and unzipped the top so Chester could poke his head out. I thought he'd like to stretch, and it would be good for him. I kept my hands on him, to be sure he didn't jump out.

While we were sitting that way, a flight attendant came down the aisle. When she saw Chester, she shrieked as if I were holding a rattlesnake. "Oh, no!" she cried. "Keep that thing away from me!"

"It's only a cat," I said. "He's very friendly."

"It's horrible!"

The passengers around us all craned their necks to see what she was carrying on about. Chester blinked his big green eyes and purred.

During the flight, Carl and I finally had time to talk, and we decided we wanted to keep Chester ourselves. "He's so mellow," I said. "He won't be a threat to Pete and Molly." We liked the idea that, by giving his cat a good home, we would be doing one final favor for Herman.

When we got home, we put Chester in the guest bedroom with a litter box and food. We wanted to introduce him to Pete and Molly gradually, to make sure that the first meeting went smoothly. I wish I could report that our efforts were successful, but here's what really happened.

Molly and Pete took one look at Chester and decided they hated him. I believe it was because he looked so much like Buddy, and they remembered the fighting that had taken place with him. For all I know, they thought Buddy had returned. Chester never had a chance to act friendly to Pete and Molly. They growled and spit while he backed away from them.

We stuck it out for three weeks, during which time we had to supervise Chester whenever he was let out of the guest room. If we didn't, he was likely to be attacked. Even when he was inside the guest room, Molly often sat in the hallway beside the closed door, glaring and hissing. I reminded her that *she* had once been the newcomer and that Pete had welcomed her, but she did not listen. We began searching for a good home for Chester.

One day when I picked up my mail at the post office, I asked the postmistress if she knew anyone who wanted a nice cat. "It needs to be a quiet home," I said, and I told her Chester's background.

She had a friend who resided in an assisted-living apartment. "She wants a cat so badly," Merrie Lou said. "Her daughter got her a kitten but it was too rambunctious and scratched her, and they had to find a new home for it. An older cat would be ideal."

It sounded like the perfect spot for Chester. I talked to the woman, and to her daughter, and we arranged to take Chester to her apartment for a visit.

I optimistically took along Chester's bed, food, and medical records, in case she loved him immediately and wanted him to stay.

I have never seen anyone so thrilled to see an animal. Her face lit up and she began talking to Chester and petting him. "He's so handsome," she said. "What a fine big boy." He sat on her lap and purred. When we went home that day, Chester stayed behind.

I called the next morning to see how he was adjusting. "You didn't need to bring that cat bed," the woman's daughter told me. "He slept with Mom last night."

Periodically, Merrie Lou reported that she'd seen Chester when she visited her friend. "That is one lucky cat," she said.

We had never talked to Herman about what should

happen to Chester if Herman couldn't take care of him any longer, but I know that by making sure Chester was loved and happy, we honored Herman's wishes.

It had been a hassle to fly a cat home with us, but it was worth it.

# I Didn't Want His Owner to Find Him

Carl and I were driving on a two-lane highway, about seven miles from our cabin. As we approached a busy intersection, the driver in front of us suddenly slammed on his brakes. We skidded to a stop, too.

A beagle, his head drooping down, plodded across the road, oblivious to the danger. Luckily, the cars coming from the other direction also saw him in time to stop. When the beagle made it safely to the far side, the car in front of us drove on. Then the dog turned around and headed back the way he had just come, crossing the highway again!

Horns honked. Brakes squealed. The dog trudged toward us, his long brown ears dragging on the pavement. Carl pulled to the side of the road while I opened the glove compartment and took out the leash we kept there. We both got out, calling, "Here, dog," coaxing the dog to come to us. The driver behind us gave us a thumbs-up as he drove past.

The leash wasn't necessary. As soon as we began talking to him, the beagle came to us. I opened the back door and the dog climbed in and settled down on the seat. He wore no collar.

An espresso stand stood on one side of the intersection and a gas station/mini-mart served the other. We went into both of them, described the dog we had picked up, and left our telephone number, in case anyone came looking for a lost dog. Then we continued toward home, making plans to take his picture and print FOUND DOG flyers to post in the area.

We'd gone only a few blocks when we heard snoring from the backseat.

The beagle, curled in a tight circle, was sound asleep.

"The poor thing is exhausted," I said. "I wonder how long he's been wandering around."

"I'm glad we don't have far to go," Carl said. "He stinks!"

I agreed, and we both cracked our windows.

At home, we put the leash on him and stood in the driveway for a closer look. "He's filthy," Carl said. "No wonder he smells bad."

"He probably has fleas, too," I said.

The beagle wagged his tail.

I got out dog shampoo and towels while Carl carried the beagle into the bathroom and put him in the tub. We poured clear water on him, and water the color of coffee ran off. We shampooed, rinsed, then shampooed and rinsed him again.

"Let's call him Willie," I suggested. I like to give animals a name quickly. Years earlier we had adopted a cat and agreed to live with her awhile before we named her. We wanted to learn her true personality so that we could choose a name that fit her character. Of course, we had to call her something in the meantime, so we called her Kitty. By the time we were ready to select a better name, she was used to Kitty and so were we. That poor cat ended up being Kitty for her whole life, a name that embarrassed me because I felt a writer ought to be more original than that.

Once Willie was clean he smelled a lot better, but the bath revealed a terrible skin condition. Large patches on his back had no fur. There were scabs where he'd scratched himself raw, and areas of flaking skin. "Maybe he has mange," I said, "or some other kind of skin disease."

"Maybe he's allergic to fleas," Carl said. As soon as Willie was dry, we put flea prevention drops on him. Then Carl vacuumed the backseat of our car.

After we saw how awful his skin was, we had second thoughts about printing up flyers to try to find Willie's family.

"Whoever owns him hasn't taken very good care of him," I said. "His skin didn't get this way in only a few days." We decided not to put up flyers after all. Instead, we would watch for LOST DOG signs and ads, to see if anyone was looking for him.

*Carl and Willie*

It was too late in the day to take him to our vet, but we didn't want to expose our own animals to a potentially contagious problem, so we decided that Willie would spend the night in Carl's workshop. The workshop, where Carl restored player pianos and other mechanical musical instruments, is attached to our house. The large space contained workbenches, supplies, shelves, cupboards, and several instruments in various stages of restoration. Windows on two sides made it bright and cheerful. That night we took Willie for a long walk and then put him in the workshop with a bowl of water, dog food, and a thick blanket to sleep on.

Beagles make a loud, baying sound, and I was afraid Willie might howl in the night, distressed at being in a strange place, but we heard nothing, not even snoring.

"He's too tired to howl," Carl said.

The next morning, I opened the door to the workshop, expecting to be greeted by an eager dog. The room was still. The blanket had been pawed into a heap, and the food bowl was empty, but I didn't see a beagle.

"Willie?" I said. I looked around. He couldn't possibly have gotten out, and he was too big to squeeze underneath one of the workbenches. "Here, Willie!" I called.

The blanket moved. Then a head poked out from underneath it. Instead of sleeping on top of the soft blanket, Willie had spent the night on the concrete floor, with the blanket heaped on top of him. He slept that way every night that he was with us.

When we found him we thought Willie was an elderly dog because of the way he trudged slowly across the road, but a bowl of dog food and a sound night's sleep perked him up and we realized he wasn't old after all.

Willie proved to be a friendly, happy dog. He liked walking on the leash and loved having his long ears rubbed. We took him to our vet, who made sure there wasn't a microchip identification. After looking at Willie's teeth, he estimated Willie was four years old. He ran some tests to try to diagnose his skin condition. "Beagles are prone to skin and coat problems," he told us, "but I think this dog has a food allergy. Let's try him on a special diet."

He gave us a medicated ointment to help heal Willie's skin and warned us not to let Willie roam free. "A beagle's nose will lead him into trouble," he said. "They're great rabbit hunters." I had a quick vision of Willie taking off into the woods after a rabbit, never to be seen again.

We bought the recommended dog food and Willie gobbled it down. Within a few days, his skin began to clear up. Two weeks later he did not look like the same dog. The ointment had worked, and the new food agreed with him. The scabs and flaky skin were gone. Thick shiny fur was growing in where Willie's bald patches had been. We bought him a stylish new collar.

Every day, I read the newspaper and craigslist notices for lost dogs but I didn't find anyone who was looking for a beagle. We returned to the gas station and espresso stand on the corner where we had found Willie. No one had inquired about a dog; there were no LOST DOG signs along the road.

"I'm glad his owners aren't looking for him," I told Carl. "If I found a LOST BEAGLE notice, I'd be honor-bound to contact that person, but I really don't want Willie to go back where he came from. He's so much healthier now."

"I don't want his previous people to have him, either," said Carl, "but we need to find him a good home."

Although we'd grown fond of Willie, we knew we couldn't keep him. We had a motor home, which we used to travel around the country while I spoke at schools, libraries, and conferences. Daisy, Pete, and Molly traveled with us. We couldn't manage another animal on those trips.

Willie needed a permanent, loving home. Our local Humane Society is a good facility but I was reluctant to take Willie there. Any animal is frightened when locked in a cage in a strange, noisy place, and it could take weeks before Willie was chosen. Still, no potential adopters were going to knock on my door unless they knew about Willie. Somehow, I needed to make that happen.

I went online, found a beagle rescue group in our area, and contacted them. I learned that they screen potential adopters carefully, and keep the dogs in foster homes until they're placed in a permanent home, no matter how long that takes. I gave them all the information I had about Willie, including his food allergy and where we had found him. I e-mailed a picture of him.

"We'd love to have him," I was told, "but we can't take him directly from you. Since he was picked up as a stray, by law he has to go to the Humane Society for three days to give his owners a chance to claim him. At the end of that time, the Humane Society will release him to us and we'll find a loving home for him. We've worked with them many times before."

I didn't like the idea of making Willie sit in a cage at the shelter for three days, but it seemed the best option, since it did guarantee that he'd be placed in a good home. We took him there late in the afternoon on day one, and the rescue group said they'd pick him up early in the morning on day three, thus fulfilling the three-day requirement while minimizing the length of time he would be at the shelter.

When we took him in, we also took the records from our veterinarian, with our names blacked out, and the bag of prescription food. I made sure the attendant understood that Willie needed a special diet. I had put all the instructions in writing so there would be no mistake.

I rubbed his ears, gave him a tearful hug, and told him good-bye. The person from beagle rescue had promised to let me know the minute Willie was released to her. The rest of the afternoon and evening dragged by as I worried about Willie feeling abandoned in a cage at the Humane Society. The next day seemed a week long.

Finally it was the morning when Willie was scheduled

to be picked up by the beagle rescue folks—but my phone didn't ring. I checked my e-mail every ten minutes. Nothing. Finally, at noon, I called my contact at the rescue group.

"Did you pick up Willie?" I asked.

"We don't have him," I was told. "His owner showed up at the Humane Society yesterday afternoon and claimed him."

My heart sank. Willie had thrived during the weeks he had lived with us. He was clean and healthy and happy— and now he was back with the owner who, I assumed, had neglected him, and there wasn't anything I could do about it. I imagined Willie's skin covered with sores again. I pictured his dirty fur, with bald patches.

"We should have tried harder to find a home for him ourselves," I said as I choked back tears. "We should never have left him at the shelter."

"We did the best we could," Carl said. "Who would have dreamed his owners were still looking for him?"

Every time we drove past the intersection where we'd found him, I felt sick inside. "I hope Willie's okay," I'd say, and Carl would nod.

Four months later, I ordered a refill of a prescription for Daisy. When I stopped at the veterinary clinic to pick it up, I got out my wallet and waited to see how much it was. "You don't owe anything," the office person told me. "You have a credit on your account of seventy-two dollars."

"That isn't right," I said. "I'd know if I had a credit, especially one that large."

She double-checked my file. "It says here that you have the credit."

Just then the vet's technician came out to the front desk. "Do you know anything about this credit on my account?" I asked.

She looked at my file and thought for a moment. "Oh, I know what that is," she said. "Remember that beagle you rescued?"

"Yes. Willie."

"Well, his owners were here. They said they'd taken him to a different veterinarian for months trying to clear up his skin problem, but nothing had helped. They were thrilled to see him in such good shape. They had the paperwork on him from the Humane Society, and it showed that we'd treated him, so they came in. They asked who had brought him to us. They were so grateful to you for helping him that they wanted to reimburse you for what you spent on him."

I'm sure my jaw was hanging open as I listened.

"We don't give out names or phone numbers of our clients," she went on, "so they asked if you were regular clients. I assured her that you bring your own animals, plus rescues, to us all the time, so they paid what you had spent on Willie and had it credited to your account."

By then I was not only grinning, I had goose bumps on my arms. "So they *did* care about Willie," I said, "but they hadn't found a vet who could solve his problem."

"Oh, they care," she said. "He dug under their fence and he'd been lost for two months, but they still checked all the area shelters every day, looking for him."

"And they found him," I said.

She nodded. "They said he had on a collar and an ID tag when he got loose. Who knows what happened to those? Now he's microchipped, in case he ever gets out again."

"I hope they kept him on the new food," I said.

"They did. In fact, they switched vets and they bring him to us now. He's doing great."

I put what seemed like my free prescription in my purse and hurried home. I couldn't wait to tell Carl that Willie was clean and healthy and loved.

# The Cats Who Had Been Shot

The beautiful calico cat crouched at the bottom of the back porch steps, watching me as I watered the pansies in my planter boxes. "Hi there, kitty," I said. "What are you doing here?"

When I started down the steps toward her, she backed away, but she moved slowly. Most feral or stray cats will run when approached; I wondered if this cat was someone's pet, or if she was sick or injured. I went inside and returned with a bowl of water and some cat food. She ate hungrily, lapped up some water, then walked off into the woods, still moving like an old person whose joints ached.

About two hours later, she returned. This time she brought three kittens with her! Two kittens were brown and gold, with white chests, the same as Mama. Kitten Three was a black-and-white tuxedo. Baby Buddy? I did some mental arithmetic and knew Buddy was not the daddy. The kittens tumbled over one another, playing in the grass while Mama cat lay in the sun. Soon the kittens began nursing.

I refilled Mama's food and water bowls and set them where she had eaten earlier. As soon as the kittens saw me, they fled back into the woods. I sat on the porch steps and waited. Mama eyed me cautiously but came to eat and drink again.

"You have beautiful babies," I told her. "I'll need to catch them and take them inside. They'll be healthier and happier if they're tame and adopted than they will be scrabbling for food in the forest. You will be, too."

Since my cats had always been spayed or neutered, I'd never raised kittens and wasn't sure how old these were, but I guessed they were four or five weeks old. I knew they needed to be socialized as soon as possible if there was any hope of taming them enough to make them adoptable.

After she ate, Mama cat stayed by the bowls, and when I slowly reached down to pet her, she let me. I stroked her thick, soft fur, and, although she didn't purr, she seemed to like being touched. When my fingers moved across her shoulder, they hit something hard. I leaned over to look more closely, and rubbed my hand across that area again. There were small, hard lumps under her skin. Did Mama have tumors? Is that why she walked slowly?

I called my vet and explained the situation. He said if I could catch her and bring her to the clinic, he'd fit her into the schedule. I went back outside, but Mama was gone, no doubt back into the woods to look after her babies.

Although I kept watching, I didn't see her again that day. The next morning when I went out to fill the bird feeders, there she was, waiting for breakfast. While she ate, I alerted Carl, and he brought the cat carrier outside. As soon as Mama finished eating, I approached her. She let me pet her again and when I picked her up, she didn't struggle.

We put her in the carrier, zipped it shut, and drove to the veterinary clinic.

Our vet examined Mama and then said he needed to X-ray the shoulder where the lumps were. While we waited, we discussed where we would put Mama and the kittens after we caught them, and decided that, once again, Carl's workshop was the best choice.

When Dr. Gran brought us the results of the X-rays, he look grim, and I braced myself for bad news. I expected him to say Mama had multiple tumors, possibly cancer. Instead he said, "This cat was shot with a pellet gun."

I gasped.

"Those lumps," he continued, "are pellets that are still inside her."

"Can you take them out?" I asked. "Should she have surgery while she's nursing kittens?"

To my surprise, he recommended leaving the pellets where they were. "Her body has healed nicely around them and they don't seem to be causing her any pain. Let's not put her through surgery unless it becomes necessary."

I looked at this lovely, trusting cat who was struggling to raise her babies in the woods. How could anyone shoot her?

I asked if the pellets might cause her to move slowly.

"More likely, she's exhausted. Until she found you, she probably hasn't had a dependable source of food, and it takes a lot of energy to nurse kittens and keep them clean."

When we got Mama back home, I longed to put her in Carl's workshop instead of turning her loose. I wanted her to have a soft, warm bed and to be safe. But I knew her kittens still needed her, so we opened the carrier in the backyard and watched as Mama slipped off into the forest again.

The next morning when I walked back to the house after getting the morning paper, I saw something by the front door. I wondered if FedEx or UPS had left a package the day before when we were gone. As I got closer to the house, I realized that the "package" was a fuzzy ball of orange, brown, black, and white fur. Mama's three kittens were curled together on my doormat, sound asleep. I felt as if Mama was telling me that she knew her babies were safe with us and that it was okay for us to help her care for them.

First we needed to corral the kittens and get them all into Carl's workshop. Mama now let me pet her any time I tried, and I knew it would be simple to pick her up again. The kittens were another matter. They scattered and hid whenever they saw me coming.

We put some kitty-num-num in a bowl on the porch for Mama and also put some in a shallow saucer near her, hoping the kittens were ready to try solid food. They were. They watched Mama eat; then they sniffed the saucer of food, took a few tentative licks, and soon devoured every crumb.

A few hours later, we put more food out, but this time instead of setting it on the porch, we put it partway down the brick path that leads from the front door of the house to the driveway and to the workshop's entrance. Each time we fed them, we put the food closer to that door, and by the next day the kittens were eating on the driveway directly outside the workshop.

The final step was to put the food inside. Before we did that, Carl tied a string to the doorknob and left the workshop door open. He laid the string across the driveway, and he sat on the far side, ready to pull on the string and jerk the door shut as soon as all four cats were inside at the same time.

*This is Mama.*
*I never got decent photos of the three kittens.*

Mama went inside and ate. One of the kittens went with her while the other two watched from the driveway. Then those two started to go in, but the first kitten ran back outside. It was like a kitten relay race and it went on for hours. They all ate, but never at the same time. One would go into the workshop; another would go tearing out. There were long stretches of time in between feedings, when none of them were inside, but Carl didn't dare leave his post for fear that he'd miss his chance.

Carl was still sitting in the driveway holding the string when the meter reader from the electric company drove in. He stopped on the far side of the string and got out, looking perplexed.

"Am I not supposed to drive across that string?" he asked.

Carl explained that the string was tied to the doorknob because he was trying to catch some feral kittens. The meter reader nodded, and gave him a look that said, "I've run into some crazy customers in my time, but this one takes the cake." Then he drove his truck across the string, got out and read the meter, and left, shaking his head.

Finally, all three kittens crowded around the food bowl at the same time. Carl yanked on the string, the door slammed shut, and the kittens were all in his workshop. Soon I caught Mama and carried her inside, too, but when I put her down in the workshop, I didn't see any kittens.

"I never knew there were so many hiding places in this room," Carl said.

"Where are the kittens?"

"One is under the workbench, one's inside that player piano, and I don't know where the third one is."

They came out when they realized Mama was there, but they kept their distance from us. It took a full week of dragging strings around for the kittens to chase, and letting them play with my shoelaces, and talking to them while they ate, before they let me touch them. I didn't get much writing done. Usually when I'm kept from writing, I get cranky, but my time in the workshop that week was a delight. There is nothing cuter or sillier than kittens.

The first time I petted one of the kittens, I got a shock. "This one's been shot, too!" I said. "I can feel the pellets in him, the same as in Mama." It made me sick to my stomach to think of someone aiming a gun and firing at these innocent little creatures. I wondered if there might have been more than three kittens in the litter. Maybe these survivors were the lucky ones.

By the end of the second week, the two calico kittens had made real progress. I still couldn't pick them up, but they let me pet them while they were eating, and they no longer ran and hid whenever one of us entered the room. The third kitten, the tuxedo, remained skittery, but I felt that, in time, he'd become tame, too.

The trouble was, our time was limited because we were scheduled to leave for Chicago in the motor home. We were attending a convention, and then I was visiting schools and giving library talks all across the Midwest. We would be gone for six weeks. Pete, Molly, and Daisy were going with us, but there was no way we could take Mama and her kittens, too. They had not yet even seen our own pets. Besides, there's a limit to how many animals I wanted to take across the United States with me.

We didn't want to leave them in the workshop even if we could find someone to come in to feed them. They needed lots more socializing, and they needed it now. When we returned in six weeks, it would be too late.

I called my friend Susan, who had founded Pasado's Safe Haven, an animal rescue group that operated a sanctuary, including a large area for cats called Kitty City. After I explained the situation, Susan offered to take all four cats. "Our volunteers will work with the kittens to finish socializing them," she said, "and then we'll try to find good homes for them. For Mama, too." I assured her that Mama was already friendly and should be adoptable as soon as the kittens were fully weaned. I arranged to bring them to Kitty City the day before we left on our trip.

Since it is a two-hour drive from the cabin to Kitty City, we decided to leave right after breakfast. We had Molly's cat carrier and the one we'd bought when we brought Chester home from Minnesota. We planned to put Mama and one kitten in the larger carrier and the other two kittens in the small one.

We put Mama in the big carrier and zipped it shut. Then we tried to catch the kittens. They seemed to know something was going to happen that they wouldn't like. I felt as if I had a sign on my shirt that said: WARNING! IF THIS PERSON CATCHES YOU, YOU'LL HAVE TO RIDE IN THE CAR FOR TWO HOURS. They hid under the workbench; they ran behind the recycle bin. Kitten Three, the one who had always been most scared, kept going inside a partially assembled player piano.

We chased those kittens for nearly an hour before we finally caught the two calicos. The tuxedo kitten was still in the piano and no amount of banging on the sides had budged him. Meanwhile, poor Mama was zipped into her carrier, waiting. We couldn't keep her confined much longer, so we decided to take Mama and the two kittens to Kitty City. Then we'd come home and continue to try to coax Kitten Three out of the piano.

"If we get him yet today, we'll make the drive again," Carl said. "If we don't, we can keep trying overnight, and take him up there first thing in the morning, on our way out of town. Worst case would be we have to hire one of the neighbor kids to come in every day while we're gone."

Off we went, with the two kittens in one carrier and Mama in the other, all three of them howling in protest. Susan had a large cage ready and waiting for them in her office, where it would be quiet. We thanked her, explained about the third kitten, and made the long drive back home.

As soon as we walked into the workshop, we saw Kitten Three dash out of the piano and hide behind some shelves, but when we tried to reach him, he escaped and returned to the piano.

"I have an idea," Carl said. "Give me a few minutes."

I was more than happy to go in the house and do something else for a while. I still needed to finish getting ready for our trip. We were leaving in the morning and I'd spent the whole day chasing after kittens.

Half an hour later, Carl came to get me. He had rigged up an old wooden organ pipe to act as a tunnel. The hollow pipe was about four inches in diameter, plenty big enough for a kitten to go into. He had one end of the pipe fastened to the piano, in the spot where the kitten always ran out. The other end of the pipe rested inside the cat carrier.

"Get ready," Carl said. "He's in the piano now but I'm going to make such a racket that he'll run into the organ pipe and out the other end. When he does, you need to close the carrier right away so he can't get out."

I knelt beside the carrier. Carl picked up an empty five-gallon paint can, held it next to the piano where the kitten was hiding, and started banging on the can with a wrench. At the same time, he yelled and stomped his feet. It was enough to make *me* want to run out of the workshop, and it worked on the kitten, too. He streaked into that organ pipe and out the other end as if he was running for his life, which I'm sure he thought he was. I yanked the end of the carrier into position and started to zip it shut, but before I got it zipped all the way, that kitten poked his head up, sprang through the opening, and ran under the workbench. I couldn't believe my eyes!

"I missed him," I said. "He went into the carrier but I didn't zip it fast enough."

To his credit, all Carl said was, "We'll have to wait until he goes back in the piano, and then try again."

"What if he doesn't go in the piano again? You scared him good."

"He's been hiding in that piano ever since he got here," Carl said. "He'll go back in sooner or later."

I fervently hoped it was sooner.

An hour passed, and then Carl came to tell me that it was time to try again.

I went back to the workshop and we both took our positions.

"Ready?" he asked.

I nodded. My heart raced. My mouth felt dry. I leaned over the carrier with one hand already on the zipper. I *had* to catch Kitten Three this time.

Carl banged on the paint can and yelled. The kitten raced into the organ pipe, and out the other end. This time, as soon as Kitten Three landed in the carrier, I tipped the carrier on its end with the open side up, and held it that way while I zipped it closed. Success!

I looked at the tiny creature who had nearly outsmarted us. He was about six inches long with wide green eyes and a halo of fuzz. His tail was the size of my pinkie finger. "This would have been a lot easier," I told him, "if you had let us catch you when we caught your siblings."

We piled into the car and made the long drive back to Kitty City. Susan greeted us with a nasty-looking red scratch that angled across her cheek from the corner of one eye almost to her mouth. "What happened to you?" I asked.

"Mama got me."

I stared at her. The cat I had assured Susan was mellow and loving had done that? "I'm so sorry," I said. "She always acted friendly with us."

Susan laughed. "She was scared to suddenly find herself in a whole new place. When I reached into the cage, I think she was defending her kittens."

"I feel as if my child has misbehaved in school," I said.

"Everyone who works in animal rescue gets scratched or bitten occasionally," Susan said.

Mama seemed overjoyed to see Kitten Three. Maybe she

had scratched Susan because she was upset that one of her babies was missing.

We left as planned the next morning. While we traveled, we often talked about Mama and her kittens, and wondered how they were doing. As soon as we got back home, I called Susan.

"All three kittens have been adopted," she told me, "but Mama is still here."

That surprised me. "Mama was the friendliest one," I said, and then added, "except for that one incident with your cheek."

Susan reminded me of what I already knew: "People want the cute little kittens. It's lots harder to find homes for older cats."

She assured me that Mama was thriving in Kitty City, enjoying the attention of the volunteers, and hurrying forward to welcome any visitors. Although she was featured on the shelter's web page and taken to off-site adoption events, no one ever chose her. I sent a case of kitty-num-num and a selection of cat toys in her honor on Mother's Day.

Eventually, Mama became the Official Greeter at Kitty City. I'm sorry that Mama never got a family of her own, but her life was far better than when she lived in the forest. She had plenty of food, a warm bed, and loving hands to stroke her fur.

# Sad Farewells

The animals brought tears as well as joy to our lives. Our beloved Daisy died, at the age of sixteen. We buried her by the blueberry bush where she used to steal blueberries out of our buckets when we were picking them.

Then one evening when we called Pete and Molly home, only Molly came. Pete had been with us on our walk an hour earlier, but he didn't come when we called, and we couldn't find him in any of his favorite places.

We didn't panic right away. We assumed he had caught a mouse and wasn't hungry for kitty-num-num. Pete had always been an independent cat who was capable of ignoring our calls while he watched us search for him.

When it got dark, we began to worry. We left all the

outdoor lights on, and circled the property with flashlights before we went to bed. I got up several times in the night, hoping to find him waiting on the porch. He wasn't there.

"Here, Pete! C'mon, Pete!" My calls drifted into the darkness, but my only answer was the hoot of an owl.

*Molly and Pete*

By morning, we were frightened. Carl spent the entire day tromping through the woods on our own property and in the forest behind us, searching for him. I am a polio survivor, and my legs are too weak to walk easily through underbrush, but I hiked along the paved road that runs in front of our place and down the old coal-mining railroad bed that's used as a public trail on the back side of our property, calling and looking.

I alerted our closest neighbors and asked them to watch for a big brown and white cat. One of them said, "Oh, we lost a cat when we first moved out here, too. We think a coyote got him." That didn't make me feel any better.

We printed posters with Pete's picture on them, and hung one on the community bulletin board at the post office where we get our mail. (There is no U.S. Postal Service delivery where I live.) We put one at the post office in a nearby small town, too. We took one to the Pierce County Humane Society, in case someone found Pete and took him there, and we left them at local veterinary clinics.

The Humane Society has a phone number to call to hear a recorded description of all animals they took in that day, including any strays they picked up. I called the number every few hours.

By evening, we feared the worst. Pete liked to sit on top of a fence post at the back of our property, near the gate. Had he jumped down on the wrong side of the fence? Had a coyote seen him and pounced? Had a dog chased him down the trail and into the woods, and now Pete was lost in the forest?

Carl continued to search every day, thinking that if a predator had caught Pete, he might at least find Pete's collar and ID tag, but he found nothing.

I listened to the Humane Society's recording every day for months. It broke my heart to think that something bad, and probably painful, had happened to Pete, and I was filled with guilt that we had not kept him indoors, where he would have been safe.

We had tried. A few years before we moved to the cabin, we had read statistics that showed indoor cats live much longer and are healthier than cats who are allowed outside. We decided to keep Pete and Molly indoors. We walked them on leashes when we traveled in the motor home, and they both seemed to like that, so we reasoned we would do the same year round.

Molly adapted right away; Pete never did. For six months, Pete spent most of his time trying to get out. He gazed longingly out the windows, often pawing at the glass, and meowing. Every time a door opened, he streaked toward the opening and tried to sneak through. No matter how often I walked him on a leash, it was never enough. He acted as if our house was a prison and his only goal in life was to escape.

We finally decided he was miserable as an indoor cat, and we let him go outside again, calling him home every night. I know Pete was happier that way, and since it didn't seem fair to let Pete go out and keep Molly in, we let her go out again, too. Of course, if we had kept Pete inside from the day we adopted him, when he was a six-week-old kitten, he would probably have been content as an indoor cat, but at that time we did not know the statistics.

*If I don't answer my mail promptly,*
*it's because Molly is sleeping in the in-box.*

I'd felt a special bond with Pete from the beginning. After our former cat, Dolly, died, at age sixteen, Carl and I had agreed to adopt a mature cat. At that time, we lived in Bellevue, Washington, and both volunteered at the Humane Society there. We knew firsthand how much harder it is to find homes for adult cats than for kittens. Dolly had been three when we adopted her, and she had been a wonderful pet.

We went to the shelter and looked at the cats, but on that

particular day we didn't see one whose paperwork said, "Good with dogs." Since we had two dogs then, it was important to us to find a cat who was comfortable around canines.

My birthday came a couple of days after that unsuccessful visit, and my friend Ginny, who later adopted Buddy, invited me to go to lunch. I passed the Humane Society on my way to meet Ginny at the restaurant, so I left home early and stopped to see if any new cats had been made available.

Pete had been brought from a foster home that morning. I took one look at Pete and all my good intentions of adopting an older cat flew out the window. I wanted that kitten! Ginny was waiting for me, so I asked the adoption staff if they could hold the kitten for me for three hours. That would give me time to have lunch, and get back to the shelter to meet Carl there, to make sure he liked this kitten, too.

It was against their policy to hold an animal without a commitment to adopt it.

I called Carl. "I'm at the animal shelter," I told him. "I know we agreed that we wouldn't take a kitten but there's one here who's the most adorable thing I've ever seen, and they won't hold him until after I have lunch and I'm afraid if I wait, he'll be gone."

I paused for breath.

"Take him," Carl said.

"You don't need to see him first?"

"I can't imagine a kitten that I wouldn't like. Remember, I didn't see George, either, until after you'd brought him home."

George was our first cairn terrier mix and, it's true, I let the kids talk me into getting him when all we'd set out to do was buy a Christmas present for our parakeet. That time I hadn't even called Carl first, but he had been delighted to come home from work and discover that a small black puppy was now part of his family. If you love animals, marry someone who loves them, too.

I told the shelter I would take Pete, paid his adoption fee, and said I'd be back to get him that afternoon. As soon as I got him home, I discovered that this adorable bit of fluff had a mind of his own and limitless energy. He climbed the drapes. He batted the pencils off my desk. He galloped up and down the stairs at night. He grabbed at the shoelaces when I tried to tie my shoes. In other words, he behaved like a kitten.

He also butted his head against us, and purred loudly whenever we petted him. He jumped on top of the player piano, and positioned himself in the middle of my Raggedy Ann doll collection. If he was hungry, he walked up and down the piano keys until he got fed. He made us laugh every single day, and I loved him wholeheartedly.

Pete lived exuberantly, seeming to relish every moment. His self-confidence and his insistence on setting his own rules were part of his charm but, in the end, they cost him his life.

About three weeks after Pete disappeared, a cat described on the Humane Society's phone recording sounded like Pete. We rushed there, but it wasn't him. The next day we held a brief memorial service for Pete and planted a tree in his memory.

Of course, we'd lost other pets over the years, and it is never easy, but my grief for Pete was different from what I felt for Daisy and for other earlier animal friends. I loved Daisy dearly, but at sixteen she had lived a full, long life. So had all of our other animals. Pete was only seven years old. He should have been with us for many more years.

Also, we knew what had happened to the others. It is terrible not to know what happened to Pete. For years, I continued to look for him. My eyes would sweep across the green of the grass and trees, hoping for a glimpse of brown and white fur, but I never saw it.

Pete was an exceptional cat, and I wanted to do something special to honor his memory. Because he often stomped around on the keyboard if I left the computer unattended for a few minutes, I had joked that he wanted to help me write my books. Several times when I left my office briefly to get a drink of water or a cup of coffee, I returned to find gibberish typed in the middle of my manuscript, and Pete sitting on my desk.

As I remembered that funny trick, I decided to write the book that I thought Pete would have written, if he could have. I began writing from Pete's viewpoint, and it felt as if Pete had miraculously returned, at least inside my head. I knew exactly what Pete would say and do, and I loved putting his thoughts on paper. Instead of crying every time I thought of Pete, I began to laugh as I imagined him swaggering about, solving a mystery. The result was *The Stranger Next Door*, by Peg Kehret and Pete the Cat.

When my publisher was ready to register the copyright for me, my editor called. "I don't think we can take out a copyright for a cat," she said. "Maybe you should not list Pete as your coauthor."

"His name has to be listed," I said. "That was the whole reason for this book."

Copyright is a protection provided to authors and others by U.S. law. When a book is copyrighted in my name, I am the only one who can give permission to make and distribute copies of it or to perform it. There are other protections, too.

An author automatically owns the copyright as soon as the book is on paper, but registering that copyright through the Library of Congress provides other legal protection and is done routinely by all publishing companies.

I doubted that anyone at the Library of Congress actually reads every application, especially those from large and well-established publishing companies who submit hundreds of copyright applications each year. I asked the editor to please request the copyright in both my name and Pete's, and see what happened.

The copyright was granted to both of us. Pete's name appears on the cover as my coauthor.

Next I wrote *Spy Cat* and later I added *Trapped*, both coauthored with Pete.

I put photos of Pete on my web site, www.pegkehret.com, for anyone who clicked "Pete's Page." Pete began to get his own fan mail. I even bought a rubber stamp of a cat with a book and used it as Pete's "pawtograph" when I signed his books.

The three Pete the Cat books are my memorial to Pete. I loved writing them and they helped to ease my sorrow. They also created a problem. My readers love Pete, too, and often ask how he is. The first time a child asked me that, I told him that Pete was no longer living, and the child burst into tears. He acted as if I'd told him that his own pet had died.

Now when anyone asks about Pete, I don't tell the truth, because it would only make them sad. Still, it seems wrong to say Pete's fine when he isn't, so now I respond by saying that Pete will always be Boss of the Universe. I hope that Pete's fans who read this will forgive me for pretending.

The real Pete became the character in the books, and now the character seems real. Pete still lives in my memory, and he lives in the minds of everyone who laughs at his antics in the books. This is what I hope for myself when I depart this Earth—to live on in the memories of those I love, and to continue to entertain readers with my books.

# The Pet I've Never Petted

I glimpsed the tabby cat in the tall grass at the rear of my property. He caught my eye because he looked so much like Molly that I had to check to be sure Molly was inside. He was there again the next day, and the next.

At the time I had begun feeding a white stray cat that I called Casper, and I realized this tabby was probably hungry, too. Casper came up on my porch to eat, and sometimes slept in one of the planter boxes that contained only dirt for the winter. The tabby was a true feral who fled if I headed toward him, no matter how far away he was. I left food and water in the area where I'd seen him, then returned to the house and watched through binoculars. He crept cautiously toward the food, ate quickly, and left.

After I'd fed Casper for a week, I set the humane trap for him. I'd made a veterinary appointment for the next morning, intending to get him (her?) spayed or neutered, and treated for any problems the vet might find, such as ear mites or fleas. I had to cancel the appointment because I didn't catch him. In fact, I never saw Casper again. I suspect his white coat made him an easy target for night-roaming coyotes, and I wish I'd tried to trap him sooner.

The feral tabby kept returning. I'd see him sitting in the tall grass, watching the house, waiting for me to bring his food. When I opened the door, he'd bolt, returning to eat only after I'd gone back inside.

I talked to him as I put the food out. "Hello, Mr. Stray," I'd say softly. "You're a good kitty. What a nice kitty, kitty. Here's your food." I hoped he would eventually associate the sound of my voice with the food and would quit running from me. Each time I put the food out for him, I set it a foot closer to the house. After two weeks, it was no longer in the tall grass, but at the edge of the mowed area. He was more visible there, so he waited until dusk to eat.

Because it rains a lot here in western Washington, I wanted to keep moving Mr. Stray's bowl until I had it on the porch. That way I could leave food out without it getting all soggy and Mr. Stray wouldn't get drenched while he had his meal. Also, I wouldn't get soaked taking the food to him.

After two more weeks I was finally able to leave the food on the back porch, where he came and ate after it got dark. There was one problem. We used the back door to let Daisy in and out. If there was any food in Mr. Stray's dish, Daisy ate it. (If there was food *anywhere*, Daisy ate it!) Also, my back door is glass and Daisy barked if she saw Mr. Stray coming up the steps onto the porch. Naturally, if the dog barked, the cat ran.

I decided I had to train Mr. Stray to come to the *front* porch. It was covered and dry, the front door was solid, and the windows on that side of the house were too high for Daisy to see out of.

*Mr. Stray, waiting for his dinner*

It was another slow process to gradually move the food off the back porch, around the side of the house, and onto the front porch, but at last we made it and Mr. Stray began to come there when he was hungry. He would sit on the small rug I'd put under his dishes and watch the window. I put a padded cat bed out for him, and he often slept in it. Whether he was asleep or awake, the second he heard the doorknob turn he leaped off the porch and either went underneath it or ran into the woods. I kept talking, though, saying, "Hello, Mr. Stray. Good, kitty, kitty," to the empty porch.

Winter arrived, and the temperatures plummeted. We decided that Mr. Stray needed better shelter. A trip to the pet store revealed lots of doghouse choices but nothing for outdoor cats. The smallest doghouses were still too big; we didn't think they'd be warm enough. We finally purchased a covered litter box made of sturdy gray plastic. The opening was big enough for Mr. Stray, but it would be snug inside.

When we got it home, Carl rigged up a customized heating system for Mr. Stray's new home. He put a heating coil in the bottom of the little house and attached it to a thermostat that hung on the outside wall. He programmed the thermostat to turn on the heating coil whenever the temperature got down to forty degrees.

We put Mr. Stray's house at the far end of the front porch, where the outside walls of the kitchen and the workshop meet. It would be most sheltered from the wind there. We positioned it so that the opening faced toward the kitchen wall. We duct-taped the seams to prevent cold air from leaking in, and draped a heavy towel over the top for added insulation. I put an old hand towel inside, and then added a small blue knitted blanket on top of the towel. Cats love knitted blankets, and I've made them for years for the shelter cats. A character in *Ghost Dog Secrets* does this, too, and instructions for the blankets are included in that book.

Next Carl drilled a hole through the side of our house! He poked the cord from the heating coil through the hole into his piano workshop, and plugged it in. A tiny red light glowed on the back of Mr. Stray's house whenever the coil was on so that we could tell without frightening Mr. Stray that the thermostat was working and his personal heating system was activated.

Mr. Stray discovered his house that same night, and he has slept in it during cold weather ever since. Often when I take food out for him early in the morning, his head will pop out of the opening and he'll watch me make my delivery. As long as I don't go too close to his house, he stays in it. Periodically when I see him outside, I remove his blanket and towel, shake them out and sometimes wash them. Once they were both so filthy that I dropped them in the garbage can and gave him new ones.

After Mr. Stray had been eating and sleeping on the front porch for a couple of months, I decided it was time to trap him. He was way too afraid of me to consider trying to find him a home, but he was a perfect candidate for Trap, Neuter and Return (TNR), a program that is intended to stop feral cats from reproducing. Cats who are not spayed or neutered have kittens at an alarming rate. If two cats produce two litters a year and the resulting cats are left to breed, too, there will be more than twelve thousand cats within five years! Cats, both feral and domestic, are healthier if they've been "fixed." I got out our trap, and made an appointment with my veterinarian to have Mr. Stray neutered the next morning.

That night we positioned the trap on the porch next to Mr. Stray's eating area. We baited it with his favorite food (kitty-num-num, naturally) and activated the trap. I peeked out the window and watched him sniff suspiciously at the trap. He walked all the way around it. He tried to reach in the closed end where the food was, but he would not enter through the open door. He went hungry that night, rather than go in the trap.

The next morning I called the vet to say I would not be bringing Mr. Stray in after all. I rescheduled for the next morning. I put fresh food in the trap and we left it set all day and another night. Again, Mr. Stray refused to go after it.

This went on for nearly a week. Later, the vet's assistant

told me they were jokingly placing bets about whether I'd ever show up to keep Mr. Stray's appointment. I never did.

A cold front moved down from Canada, bringing us nine inches of snow. I couldn't bear to see Mr. Stray go without food in such cold weather, so I put the trap away and gave him free access to his meals again. He devoured the food, then settled into his warm house. The score was: Mr. Stray 1, Peg 0.

Over the years, I've tried several more times to trap Mr. Stray but I have never succeeded. The score is now Mr. Stray 7, Peg 0. My hunch is that he had been trapped at some time in the past, and he is too wily to repeat such a frightening experience.

I've always regretted that I have not been able to provide veterinary care for him. Twice I purchased worm medication from the vet and mixed it in his food. Both times, he refused to eat it. It sat on the porch until it got rotten, when I threw it away. I'd like to put flea treatment on him, but I can't get close enough to do that.

I'm not even positive that he is *Mr.* Stray. Perhaps he is *Ms.* Stray, although it seems likely that he is a male cat because in the eleven years that he's been eating and sleeping on my porch, there's never been a litter of kittens. He doesn't spray, as many unaltered male cats do, and he doesn't fight with Dillon, my neighbor's male cat who visits now and then.

In *The Ghost's Grave*, the cat character is a combination of Mama cat and Mr. Stray. In the book, she's called Mrs. Stray.

He no longer hides from me, but he stays at least six feet away. He still has his padded cat bed in addition to his house, and he often naps there in the late morning sun. If I open the door when he's sleeping, he leaps out of the bed and watches warily from farther down the porch.

A few months after Daisy died, we adopted Lucy from a rescue group. She is a cairn terrier, the same as Daisy, but with a whole different look and personality. Daisy was mellow; Lucy gets hyper. Daisy was brindle color; Lucy's fur is reddish tan. Daisy was quiet; Lucy barks too much.

Lucy has chased Mr. Stray many times. When this happens, he always runs to the tree house that Carl built for our grandchildren, climbs the ladder, and sits on the tree house floor, staring down as Lucy barks, sniffs, and runs around at the base of the ladder.

I always look before I let Lucy out, and try not to turn her loose if Mr. Stray is nearby, but I don't always see him if he's in the tall grass, or sitting behind a tree. A low wooden barrier keeps Lucy away from Mr. Stray's part of the porch, so she can't eat his food or surprise him when he's sleeping in his bed or his house. I think Lucy could easily jump over the barrier, but she's never tried to do so.

I am certain that being chased by a dog, even a dog as small as Lucy is, has kept Mr. Stray cautious and hindered my attempts to tame him. Lucy may be little, but she makes a lot of noise.

Even though I never let Lucy out with me when I'm taking Mr. Stray his food, she often woofs while I'm out there because she hears me talking to him and thinks a person has come. Of course, Mr. Stray hears her. Even though she's in the house, I know it makes him uneasy.

I have made some progress; he often answers me now, when I talk to him.

"You're a fine cat," I tell him.

*"Mrow,"* he'll say.

"What a good kitty."

*"Mrow, mrow."*

"Here's your food, Mr. Stray."

*"Mrow."*

I've noticed he's most inclined to talk to me when he's hungry, so all of our conversations occur when I am delivering his meals.

When I consider how many potential hazards there are in Mr. Stray's life, I marvel that he has lived this long. On the other side of my fence, there are coyotes, cars, large dogs, an occasional bobcat, and, possibly, cruel people. A stray cat faces danger every second. My hope is that he doesn't wander off my property much, and I suspect this is the case.

He is a good hunter, and occasionally leaves a dead mouse on the doormat, as my thank-you gift. He has even caught moles. He eats all except their wicked-looking front claws, and their heads. Those he leaves for me to find and bury.

Mr. Stray recognizes me. When I look out the window, to see if he's waiting at his food station, I can tell that he knows it's me. Occasionally, I've had a guest look out that window when he is there, and he always runs off when he sees a face other than mine. He even recognizes my car! If I am out in the evening and get home later than when he's usually fed, he'll show up on the front porch before I even get my coat off.

Mr. Stray appears to be healthy and content. I know that a steady diet of high-quality food, along with a safe and warm place to sleep, are the reasons he is doing so well. He has not had to venture away from my property, where so many dangers lurk, to find food. He hasn't had to spend nights unprotected from the snow and rain.

I still hope that someday I'll be able to pet him. I'd like

him to feel the touch of loving hands, and to be happy and relaxed enough to purr.

Realistically, that may not ever happen. Like so many things in life, I can't control the outcome of my efforts. All I can do is to feed him, to keep him as safe and comfortable as possible, and to keep talking to him. If this results in my being able to pet him eventually, I will be thrilled. If it doesn't, I still have the satisfaction of knowing that I helped him. Eleven years is a long time for a feral cat to survive; I doubt if Mr. Stray would have made it without me.

# Living with Wildlife

When we first settled into our cabin in the forest, I began keeping a journal of wildlife sightings. I recorded the date and what I'd seen, for no reason other than, as a writer, I tend to write things down.

We knew we would be living with deer, but we had not expected elk. They are huge animals. They came single file along one of the deer trails, jumped over a low area of the fence, and grazed only a few yards from the house. The first time I saw a bull elk with a five-foot rack of antlers standing within a few yards of my window, I got chills.

The elk are alert to noise and movement. They get spooked more easily than the deer do and, when that happens, they crash off into the woods like bulldozers, trampling whatever's in their path. Since they often arrive at sunset, we learned to turn off all the lights in the house while we watched them, so that they didn't see us, and to hold Lucy so she wouldn't bark.

*Elk*

In a few years my wildlife journal proved useful because I realized the animals follow the same cycle, season after season. It didn't matter whether we'd had a frigid winter with a lot of precipitation, or a mild, dry one, the elk migrated through our property within a day or so of April sixth, on their way up the mountain where they spend the summer.

They are usually here in the evenings or early in the morning, for two or three weeks.

*This is Lucy after she rolled in elk poop.*
*She knows she's about to get a bath.*

They return in September. They do a lot of damage to my trees every time they come, especially the younger trees that we planted in our first years here. They strip the branches of leaves, reaching their heads seven or eight feet up to eat. They knock whole branches off the fir trees, and ruin big patches of bark when they rub their heads against the tree trunks. Despite all the damage, I'm always glad when they come, because I never tire of watching them.

Unfortunately, Lucy loves the smell of elk poop. When she finds a pile of it, she instantly flops down and rolls on it. Then she trots over to me with gooey black streaks on both sides of her neck and down her back, looking all pleased with herself as if to say, "Aren't I lovely? Smell my new perfume!" Lucy gets a lot of baths during elk season. Daisy used to do the same thing.

Carl designed birdhouses and helped our grandkids build and hang them. We learned to distinguish between the tapping sounds of a flicker and those of a pileated woodpecker. Yellow goldfinches, Washington's state bird, brighten the feeders. Their deep yellow feathers, accented with black, seem to glow in the sunlight.

The blue jays throw the most seed to the ground. Those jays have no table manners. They shake their heads as they peck the seed, sending more seed flying to the ground than what they eat. Fortunately, the mourning doves are ground feeders who come to clean up the mess. Of all the bird sounds, I like the *coo, ah, coo-coo-coo* of the mourning doves best.

Eagles, both golden and bald, come infrequently, so it's always exciting to spot one. An occasional red-tailed hawk tries to use the feeders as a diner, preying on the small birds, but they know when a hawk is around, and they disappear until he leaves.

We came home after dark one night and spotted a porcupine waddling across the lawn. Another day, we saw two martens. Anne and I once saw a mountain beaver.

My journal proved useful in knowing when to fill my hummingbird feeder and hang it outside for the summer. Like the elk, the hummingbirds follow a pattern and I can now predict within a day when I will see them. I find it interesting that the largest creatures I see on my property and the smallest both follow some sort of internal clock that regulates when they migrate.

One day as I walked on my nature trail, a flurry of feathers exploded from the forest floor beside me. I got only a glimpse of the bird as it flew into the woods. It was the size of a chicken with coloration that made it blend perfectly with its habitat. I consulted my bird books and identified a ruffed grouse.

I saw it only once more that summer when I was walking, although I always watched carefully in that part of the woods. Then one afternoon I stood up from my desk to stretch, looked out my office window, and saw a ruffed grouse with a brood of chicks! She herded them along the edge of the tall grass. After they had gone a few feet, they all returned to their mother who spread her wings and gathered the chicks underneath. She sat still for about a minute before all the chicks emerged again and repeated the process of walking forward and then returning. I assumed it was a training exercise where the chicks were learning to explore on their own, but also being taught to return to Mom when she gave the signal.

Sometimes the deer get frisky. A group of five or six deer will jump in the air, kick up their heels, and race in circles. I call it the Dancing Deer Revue. The show usually lasts about fifteen minutes.

*Cats aren't the only ones who are curious.*

The deer are curious. One day Molly was dozing in the warm grass while I watched her from the porch. A deer approached, her ears perked forward, and slowly stepped closer to Molly. The deer was so curious about the cat that she stayed when I stood up and aimed my camera at her.

Molly clearly didn't feel threatened; she calmly watched the deer move within two feet of her. When I took a photo, the shutter sound caused the deer to leave. I've watched deer try to sneak close to Mr. Stray, too, and they do the same thing at night with 'possums.

Birds can also be curious. My closest neighbor, Chris, raises peacocks, and when I was having a new roof put on the cabin, she called to say that the peacocks were curious about all the noise. Usually, my place is quiet, but the roofers were pounding and banging, and Chris said the peacocks kept trying to peek through the trees to see what was going on.

About an hour after Chris phoned, here came the Peacock Patrol: four males, one female, and one guinea hen. They rarely come in my yard, but they headed straight toward the cabin as if they came to call every day. They lined up in a row, parallel to the house, and stared at the roof. The roofing crew thought it was hilarious. The birds watched for a few minutes, then turned and marched back home with their curiosity satisfied.

Although I was not officially enrolled in a college course, I felt as if I was taking Wildlife 101 because each new bird or animal that I spotted sent me to the library or online to learn more. I made notes from my own observations, too, and when I chatted with people who lived nearby, the talk often turned to the forest critters. I learned many fascinating facts. For example, ruffed grouse grow comblike projections off the sides of their toes in winter. These act as snowshoes, helping the grouse walk in snow.

*The visiting peacocks*

We often saw 'possums around the bird feeders at night. Their real name is opossum, but I've chosen to write the word the way most people pronounce it. I watched them climb the feeder post, using their prehensile tails for balance while they ate the seed. Prehensile tails can wrap around and grasp an object—a useful trait when you're perched on the edge of a bird feeder, eating seeds. 'Possums are the only animal in North America to have pouches. Like the kangaroos in Australia, female 'possums carry their newborn in a pouch.

I like their pointed pink faces and their tiny pink paws, but when I mention 'possums to other people, I find that I am in the minority when I think they are cute. I have heard far too many roadkill jokes. It's true that 'possums are not the most intelligent of animals. They move slowly, and when they see oncoming headlights, they freeze in place instead of running to safety. Even so, I feel a fondness for these creatures that most people consider ugly. To even things out, I included a rescued 'possum in *Spy Cat*, hoping I might encourage a few readers to be tolerant of them.

Using my bird books, I have tried to identify all of the guests at the feeders. The biggest of these are the band-tail pigeons, who arrived the first year in flocks of thirty or more. It was hard to count them because they moved around so much, but I got up to thirty-four one day and was fairly certain I had not counted any bird twice. Band-tails are slate gray, with a thin crest of white on top of their necks. The "band" in their name is a black stripe on the underside of their tails that shows when they are in flight.

My son-in-law, Kevin, calls them the B-29s, after the four-engine propeller-driven airplanes that the United States used in World War II and the Korean War. The B-29s were big, too, and gray, and loud. The first atomic bomb was dropped from a B-29.

The band-tail pigeons are the clowns in my yard, never

failing to entertain me. They flap their wings noisily as they crowd onto the feeder, sitting on its roof as well as on the side perches. In their eagerness to get their portion, they even stand on top of each other! They flutter and flap, trying to keep their balance as they push each other off. Displaced pigeons fly to the house roof or the porch railing, rest a moment, and then return to jostle for position at the feeder.

Band-tail pigeons are wild, native birds and are not the same as the pigeons that are often seen in cities and parks. Those pigeons actually are rock doves and were imported from Europe. Band-tails are between fourteen and seventeen inches long and weigh about a pound. They sit high up in the trees—I often see them on the topmost branches of the conifers—where they make a low cooing sound. Band-tail pigeons are known to return to the same nest site each year. They mate for life and, in this part of the country, raise only one young per year.

One day I saw a newspaper article that announced a hunting season for band-tail pigeons, the first in many years. When I researched this, I learned that the band-tail pigeon population had been so severely reduced by hunting and by heavy harvesting of trees in the low-elevation forests that hunting them had been prohibited for many years. Now their numbers had increased, so the hunting ban had been lifted.

Band-tail pigeons are about a third of the size of a

duck—hardly enough meat to be worth the trouble. I talked one day with a man who hunted them, and I asked how he cooked them. "Oh, I don't eat them," he said. "I leave the ones I shoot for the coyotes or other scavengers to find."

It seems to me there are better ways to have target practice than killing birds.

The following summer, after band-tail hunting had been legal for a year, my flock was much smaller than before. Instead of three dozen band-tails at a time, I had only six or seven.

I worried that the band-tails would suffer the same fate that had befallen the passenger pigeons. In the early 1800s, there were an estimated three to five billion passenger pigeons in eastern North America. They were the most abundant bird species ever. Eyewitness accounts tell of flocks so large that they "blackened the sky" for hours as they flew over.

Due mostly to overhunting and to the clearing of forests, passenger pigeons are now extinct. The last known passenger pigeon in the wild was shot in 1900. The last one in captivity died fourteen years later in the Cincinnati Zoo.

Passenger pigeons had lovely red breasts and long tail feathers. They were once our most common bird, but we will never again see one alive.

I wrote to the State Fish and Wildlife Department, the agency that decides hunting regulations, and told them about the swiftly declining band-tail population in my area. I requested that these birds be protected again, with a ban on hunting them. That didn't happen, but the state does limit how many band-tails can be killed each year. (The hunting guides never use the word *killed*. They say *harvested*.) Now the numbers remain fairly stable from year to year, so I'm hopeful that the band-tails will be around for a long, long time.

I also enjoy watching the little juncos as they go about their bird business. One day I saw one of them pecking at the carpet square that Mr. Stray's food sits on. I thought it was eating dried bits of spilled cat food. Then I saw that the junco was tearing out tiny tufts of carpet fiber and using them to build a nest.

I wanted to help with this effort, so I brushed Lucy and Molly, and put their fur out on the porch. The juncos immediately took it for nesting material. A friend puts dryer lint out for the birds, but I have more pet fur than dryer lint. I brush the animals most days anyway; when it's nesting time, I toss the excess fur outside.

The juncos are a busy bunch, including the one I call Yo-Yo Bird. For the last two springs, while the rest of the juncos are building their nests, this one bird flies up from a shrub to the top of a garage window and back down, a distance of about four feet. He does it over and over, all day long, from the same branch on the bush to the same spot on the window molding. While the other juncos collect materials and construct nests, this one simply goes up and down like a yo-yo.

That junco resembles a few people I know who rush around doing trivial chores but never accomplishing anything.

My favorite birds are the California quail. I currently have a covey of five who live in a brush pile at the back of my property. Several times daily they trot single file toward the bird feeder that's nearest my back porch. The males have a distinctive black topknot that bobs up and down as they scratch for seed. The females' topknot is smaller, and their coloring is not as vivid.

Most quail coveys are much larger than mine, averaging around fifty birds. The quail watch out for each other. When one finds a source of food, it usually calls to the rest, to share the bounty. A "guard" often perches in a high spot to watch for predators while the rest of the birds eat. If it perceives danger, it warns the others. California quail communicate with fourteen different calls.

The first snow after we lived in the cabin brought surprises. When I walked down the driveway to get the morning paper, I found lots of animal tracks, including rabbit tracks which led to a secluded den that I hadn't known existed, in a fallen tree. Deer tracks crisscrossed the driveway, and there were some small tracks that I did not recognize.

*Deer in the snow*

I bought a book that identified various animal tracks and consulted it often through the years. The tracks that I didn't recognize that first morning in the snow turned out to be mice! Even the birds leave tracks in the snow. Bird tracks are usually in pairs, because the birds don't walk, they hop.

One summer the deer began to look scruffy. Soon they had big bald patches, where their fur had fallen out. I found clumps of their fur on the ground, and I watched them scratch at themselves with their hind hooves, the way a dog will scratch at a flea bite. Their condition got worse and worse as the summer progressed.

I contacted the wildlife department and learned that the herd had deer hair-loss syndrome. Most of western Washington's blacktail deer population was afflicted that year. Deer hair-loss syndrome is caused by lice and it impacts the animal's overall health, often getting so severe that the deer dies.

I asked if there was any medication to cure it. I thought perhaps I could put pills in apples and leave them out for the deer to eat. I was told that the only remedy had to be injected, which made it impossible for wild deer.

One fawn had a particularly bad case. I watched helplessly as the fawn lost more and more hair and clearly became weaker. We had a cold spell, and the fawn was nearly bald. One day I realized I had not seen the fawn in over a week. It never came again; I'm sure it died of the hair-loss syndrome.

The deer often bed down in the tall grass behind my house to bask in the sun and chew their cuds. One summer day, the year after the hair-loss problem, I saw a large doe walk to a sunny spot and settle into the grass. Usually, two or three deer rest together, but this one was by herself.

I was in my office, writing, and periodically I glanced out the window to see if she was still there. She was. After a couple of hours had passed, I looked out just as she stood up—only she was no longer alone. Twin fawns on wobbly legs stood beside her! The doe washed her babies, and they began to nurse.

*The deer is napping in front of my house,*
*next to my driveway.*

They were much smaller than the fawns we'd seen in previous years, less than two feet tall, and frail looking. Maybe they were so tiny because they were twins or perhaps it was only because they were newborns. After the mother deer finished nursing them, she led them into the woods and I didn't see them again for two weeks. By then, they had doubled in size.

Fawns are kept hidden when they're tiny. Because they are earth-colored, with white spots that look like dappled light, they are hard to see when they're curled in a tight ball, under a low-growing plant. I was fortunate to have seen these when they were so small.

I've seen baby elk here, too. Those babies are the size of a year-old deer.

Well-meaning people sometimes find a hidden fawn and, assuming it is orphaned, take it home with them. This is the wrong thing to do. The fawn's mother is almost always close by and, once the humans leave, she will return for her baby. It's best, if you should ever come across a hidden fawn, to leave it alone. Don't touch it. Just leave the area quickly and quietly.

A second set of fawns was born nearby that year, although I was not lucky enough to see them until they were older. Perhaps the twins were Nature's way of making up for the young deer who died the year before of hair-loss syndrome.

*Fawn*

One day I found a snake skin in the woods. The skin of a snake does not grow as the snake grows, so when the snake has outgrown its skin, it sheds the outer layer. This happens many times over a snake's lifetime.

I found the skin of a garter snake, about sixteen inches long. It was intact, including the head. I had never seen a snake skin outside of a museum, so I was excited to have such a treasure. The brittle paper-thin tube looked exactly like a hollow snake.

After the old skin has been sloughed off, the snake's new skin is smooth and colorful. When I look at all the wrinkles I've accumulated on my face as I age, I think the snakes may have the right idea.

I didn't want to keep the snake skin in the house because I feared Molly might attack it, so I displayed it on a small shelf in Carl's workshop.

I decided from the start not to feed the wild animals. I didn't want them to become tame, which would make them more vulnerable during hunting season, and I thought it was best for them not to get dependent on humans for their food.

However, one winter we had particularly severe weather. Normally it snows here once or twice each winter, the snow lasts a couple of days, and then we return to our normal rainy winter weather. That year, it snowed often, and the temperatures were so cold that the snow didn't melt.

The deer began to seem desperate in their foraging and started eating plants around the house that they had never touched before. They grew so thin that I could clearly see their ribs.

By then, I knew that there are state regulations against feeding deer, but those rules were to discourage the practice of "baiting," where food is regularly left in the same place, to encourage the deer to come there so that they are easily hunted. Feeding them to help them through a harsh winter seemed okay. I went to the local feed store and purchased a forty-pound bag of cracked corn. "Going to feed some deer?" the clerk asked.

"Yes." I wondered if he was supposed to report anyone who fed wild deer.

"You aren't the only one. Lots of people are taking pity on them this year."

I was glad to hear that. Back home, I put out a tin washtub filled with cracked corn, and the deer lost no time in finding it. I continued to keep it filled until the weather improved, when I let the deer fend for themselves again.

Without intending to, I feed two of the does year-round. They have learned to stand on their hind feet, crane their necks up, and lick the sunflower seeds out of the bird feeders! It is quite a balancing act, and I'm sure they expend more energy getting those seeds than the seeds provide when they're eaten.

Kevin mounted the feeders on taller poles to discourage

those deer, but they can still reach the seed. If the feeders were any higher, I wouldn't be able to refill them. I also planted flowering shrubs around the base of the feeders, thinking that would force the deer to stay back. Instead, they ate the shrubs.

One day when I was making applesauce, I looked at the pile of apple peels and cores in my sink and thought what a treat they would be for the deer. It seemed wasteful to let them rot in my garbage can when they could provide nourishment for the deer, so I gathered up all the apple peels and scattered them outside. Later I saw the deer discover the treat and when I checked the next morning, every piece was gone.

Since then, I always give the deer lettuce cores, the ends of carrots, and watermelon rinds. I throw the produce in a different area each time so that the deer don't return to a specific place for their treats. I want them to come across it in the natural course of their grazing so they don't associate it with humans.

Man is the principal enemy of all wild creatures. If I can shift the balance a bit by leaving a few fruits and vegetables for the deer to find, I'm happy to do it.

# My Life Changed Forever

*N*ot every chapter in my life has had a happy ending. Sometimes tragedy strikes, and there's nothing we can do to prevent it.

Carl was born with a faulty heart valve. It did not cause a problem until he was in his fifties, and when it did, he treated the symptoms for a long time with medication. Eventually his condition became serious, and surgery was the only hope of correcting it. He was an excellent candidate for heart surgery—slender, physically fit (except for the heart problem), and he had never smoked. The cardiologist felt confident that the surgery would give Carl many additional years of a productive life.

We entered the hospital feeling optimistic, and I stayed with him while he was prepped for surgery. This included being washed with an antiseptic. When it was time for the nurse to take him into surgery, I asked if it was okay to kiss him.

It was. He was hooked up to a heart monitor, and I joked that we would make the monitor jump. I gave him a quick good-luck kiss.

"I love you," he said.

"I love you, too."

I spent the next eight hours in a waiting room. My daughter, Anne, and her husband, Kevin, waited with me. Three times, a nurse called me from surgery to give me an update. First the surgeon tried to repair the faulty valve. When the repair didn't work, he replaced the valve. Finally— finally!—I got a call that the new valve was working, they were sewing Carl back up, and I could see him in the recovery room in about half an hour.

What joy! Relief flooded through me as I hugged Anne and Kevin and told them the happy news.

Since we'd been too anxious all day to eat, we decided to stop at the hospital cafeteria for a quick lunch before heading to the recovery room. I had just put a sandwich on my tray when I heard my name being paged. I was asked to report to the Intensive Care recovery room.

I left Anne and Kevin to deal with our food, and rushed to the elevator. A nurse met me with devastating news. "Something went terribly wrong," she told me. "We've coded him, and it doesn't look good." She showed me where to wait, and I asked her to page Anne and Kevin. They arrived almost immediately, and we clung to one another. In less than ten minutes, we had gone from relief and joy to the most intense fear I've ever felt.

Soon the doctor came out. As soon as I saw his face, I knew. "I'm sorry," he said. "A hole burst in his aorta, and we couldn't save him."

After forty-eight years of marriage to my dearest friend, he was gone.

I had been living an ideal life and now, suddenly, that life had changed drastically and would never again be the same.

As I endured the months of deep grief, I had to make decisions. I chose to stay in my log cabin in the woods. I feel close to Carl here, in the dream home that we built together, and I hoped that the peacefulness of my surroundings would help restore tranquility to my heart. Besides, I told my family, I can't move because who would take care of Mr. Stray?

I sold the motor home. I cherish my memories of the many trips we made to schools, libraries, and conferences, but I knew I would not drive it cross-country alone. I wept as the dealer drove it out of my driveway. I had removed the custom license plate, BKS4KDS (Books For Kids), and it now hangs on the wall in my bathroom. My entire home is filled with mementos of happy times, even the bathrooms.

Carl's workshop presented more of a challenge. From the day we moved in, the workshop had been filled with the antique musical instruments that he restored. Old sheet music, much of which belonged to my grandmother, hangs on the walls.

"Listen to this," Carl would say as he cranked a vintage cob organ or pumped a 1920s player piano. Music floated above the workbench, and the room was alive with purpose.

When Carl died, he had several projects under way, including an expensive music box that he had agreed to restore for a museum. He had taken it completely apart and left the pieces spread across the workbench, intending to begin the restoration while he recovered from heart surgery. I looked at all those parts and dreaded calling the museum that owned the music box.

For many years, we had belonged to the local chapter of AMICA, Automatic Musical Instrument Collectors Association, and our good friends in that group came to my rescue. Ron Babb took all the pieces of the music box home with him. He told me that Carl had once helped him restore that same type of music box, so he knew exactly what to do.

Ron not only got the music box working, he delivered it to the museum for me.

Mark Smithberg completed another of Carl's unfinished projects, and Kurt Morrison helped sort through the contents of shelves and drawers. One by one, the instruments left. After I gave the extra piano strings, bolts of felt, tools, and other supplies to these helpful friends, I was left with an empty workshop. Now the walls enclosed only memories.

One day I stood in the silent, barren room with tears dripping down my cheeks and questions tumbling in my mind. What should I do with this space?

I didn't need another bedroom or any additional living space, but I couldn't bear to think that the room would go unused. I had turned the heat off when the last instrument left, and now the cold seeped through my sweater and into my bones. How could I make Carl's workshop a cheerful place again? How do I rebuild my life?

As I recalled the many happy times we'd had in that room, an image of Willie flashed across my mind, and I smiled as I thought of the beagle sleeping on the cold concrete floor, underneath his warm blanket. Then I remembered how hard it had been to tame Mama's wild kittens, and the organ pipe Carl had used to trick the third kitten into the carrier.

A seed of an idea took root in these memories. From

my involvement with animal rescue groups, I knew there is a constant need for foster homes for rescued animals. Shelters always have animals who need individual socialization, or a quiet place to recover from surgery or who, for myriad other reasons, would benefit from staying temporarily in a foster home. I dried my tears, and decided to turn the piano workshop into a foster home for cats.

Despite my happy memories of Willie, and the fact that I've always had a dog, I limited my foster efforts to cats. I used to volunteer at adoption events in a local shopping mall where I helped display and talk about shelter animals who were ready for adoption. I'd had to give up that volunteer activity when weakness from post-polio syndrome made it difficult for me to carry and set up the cat cages and to handle the large dogs. Most abandoned and rescued dogs are big. When taken to a new place, they get excited, and, sometimes, unruly.

I contacted Susan at Pasado's Safe Haven and offered to take a foster cat. Two days later, Edgar arrived. I had never seen such a terrified animal. A black cat with big yellow eyes, Edgar had been at the Kitty City sanctuary for two weeks. Despite the efforts of volunteers, he hid all the time and didn't eat. Edgar was afraid of everything and everyone.

"He is not adoptable as he is now," I was told. "We hope you'll be able to help him relax and learn to trust people."

As soon as we let him out of the carrier, Edgar squeezed underneath Carl's workbench and refused to come out. For days, I spent hours each day lying on my stomach beside the workbench, talking softly and trying to coax him out. I put dried salmon and canned tuna and other treats next to him. He cowered against the back wall and stared at me.

When I was out of the room, he came out to eat and use the litter box, but he scurried back to his hiding place whenever I returned. I took a radio to the cat room and left it on low volume for a couple of hours each day, hoping he'd get used to normal household sounds. I brought a book with me and sat by the workbench to read so that he'd get used to my presence and not feel threatened. I talked to him often, but he gave no sign that he was listening.

*Edgar*

One morning when Edgar had been with me about two weeks, I went into his room and saw him sitting on top of a cupboard. Instead of leaping down and hiding, as he always had before, he remained where I could see him. A few days later, he waited on the floor while I put fresh food in his bowl.

Finally the day came when he let me pet him. A few days after that, I was sitting in the chair one afternoon, reading, when Edgar came and stood beside me, looking up. I realized he was thinking about jumping into my lap.

I set the book down. "Come on, Edgar," I said, patting my knees. "Get up here."

He jumped into my lap. I stroked his back, and soon he began to purr. I felt like cheering! The sound of a cat purring is a happy sound under any circumstances. Knowing Edgar's background, the purr was especially welcome.

Once he decided he was safe, Edgar blossomed. He began to play with his toys, batting the catnip mice around and leaping after the feather-on-a-stick. He let me pick him up. He followed me around when I cleaned his room.

I introduced him to Lucy, thinking he would be more adoptable if I could say he got along with my dog. First I put a baby gate in the doorway so that Lucy and Edgar could see each other but still be separated. After a couple of days of letting them eye one another through the gate's plastic mesh, I let Lucy into the cat room. She acted a little scared of Edgar, and he ignored her at first. Soon they sniffed noses and from then on, they were pals. Lucy wagged her tail whenever she saw him, and Edgar would try to rub up against her. Sometimes they curled up together in Edgar's bed and had a nap.

Molly wanted no part of it. She had decided long ago, first with Buddy and then with Chester, that she would not tolerate the addition of any more cats to the household. When she saw Edgar through the baby gate, her tail whipped back and forth, and she hissed at him. Many times when I'd reenter the main part of the house from the cat room, I'd find Molly standing next to the door with her fur puffed up, clearly outraged by my disloyalty.

Except for when there was another cat in the house, Molly was a sweet, shy cat who never caused a bit of trouble. I had promised myself I would not adopt any of the foster cats because if I did, I wouldn't be able to continue as a foster parent. Since Edgar was not going to stay permanently, I decided Molly did not need to adjust to him, and I simply kept them apart.

I sometimes shut Molly in a bedroom and let Edgar explore the whole house. He was a curious cat who jumped up on all the furniture and poked his nose into every corner. Every morning I had to hunt for the toys I'd left out the night before. During the night, he batted them behind cupboards, under the workbench, and beneath the recycle bin.

Whenever I had guests, I asked them to spend a few minutes in the cat room with Edgar so that he'd get used to other people. Since all of my friends are animal lovers, they were happy to oblige. Slowly Edgar learned to trust other people and eventually my friends could hold him and pet him. Two of my grandkids visited while Edgar was here and spent a lot of time playing with him. Once again, Carl's workshop was filled with life and laughter.

Of course I fell completely in love with Edgar and wanted to keep him, but that would have defeated my purpose. Anyone who volunteers to help animals knows that you can't keep them all. It was more important to find a loving permanent home for Edgar, and then use Carl's workshop to foster another needy cat.

*Edgar, my first foster cat, in his permanent home
with his friend Lacy*

When Kitty City participated in a cat adoption event at a pet store, I took Edgar and spent the day talking to prospective adopters. A wonderful woman named Heather came in looking for a cat who would be a companion for her dog, Lacy, while she was at work. When I mentioned that Edgar got along well with my dog, she went out to her car and brought Lacy in to meet Edgar. The two animals sniffed noses and then calmly looked at Heather as if to say, "Now what?"

I told her how scared Edgar had been at first, and how loving and friendly he was now. She decided he was exactly the cat she wanted. Heather filled out the adoption application, a volunteer from Pasado's did a home visit, and a few days later Heather arrived to take Edgar home.

Edgar had been here for six months, and I felt sad to see him leave, but it was not the tender good-bye that I had anticipated. After all my bragging about how friendly he was, Edgar hid under the workbench when Heather entered the room and refused to come out! I had to lie on the floor, reach under the workbench, drag him out by one leg, and stuff him into the carrier.

First, Mama had scratched Susan after I claimed Mama was tame. Now Edgar hid from the woman who had adopted him after I'd told her how friendly he was. If this kept on, nobody would believe anything I said.

As I waved good-bye to Heather, I felt a deep sense of satisfaction that I had helped Edgar overcome his fears and find a wonderful new life. Heather sends me frequent updates and photos of him. My favorite shows Edgar and Lacy, the dog, lounging together on Heather's bed.

That night I cleaned the cat room, washed out the litter pan, and put away the toys. (Edgar's favorites had gone home with him.)

The next morning, a woman who lives half a mile down the road knocked on my door. "A kitten followed me home from my walk," she said. "I have no idea where it lives. I tried to shoo it away but it kept coming. Can you take care of it?"

She had brought the kitten to me because I had called her once to tell her about Edgar, hoping she and her husband might want a cat. They didn't, but my call had alerted her to the fact that I helped homeless animals. Once you establish that reputation, you can be sure of getting requests for help with many unwanted dogs and cats.

The adorable brown and white kitten looked a lot like Pete; I felt certain I'd be able to find a home for him. I turned the heat back on in the cat room, and Charlie moved in. I posted FOUND KITTEN signs around the neighborhood and made numerous phone calls asking if anyone knew of a lost kitten.

Unlike Edgar when he arrived, Charlie was already friendly and loving. He had clearly been around people. He had no identification tag, and a scan showed no microchip. My veterinarian estimated that Charlie was four months old.

Late that afternoon, Mark Smithberg, who is like a second son to me, came out to visit and to help me with some heavy chores. Mark and I often stay up far too late working a jigsaw puzzle and, since it's a long drive from his house to the cabin, we had planned for him to spend the night in my guest room.

As soon as he got here, I took him out to the cat room to meet Charlie. Mark had met Edgar several times and did not intend to adopt a cat, but when he picked Charlie up, Charlie put his front paws around Mark's neck in a hug, and began to purr. Mark instantly decided he needed a pet!

We moved the litter box from the cat room to the guest bedroom so that Charlie could spend the night with Mark. The next morning, we took down the FOUND KITTEN signs. None of my phone calls had produced any leads. When Mark went home, he borrowed Molly's carrier, and Charlie went with him.

Mark told me later that Charlie is afraid of cardboard boxes, so I suspect Charlie was part of an unwanted litter and was put into a box, driven out in the country, and abandoned.

Unwanted animals are often dumped in rural areas. Some people mistakenly believe that domestic animals will remember the survival skills of their ancestors and get along on their own, but that doesn't happen. Most abandoned animals starve, get hit by cars, or are killed by predators. Charlie got lucky.

*Me in the doorway of the cat room,*
*holding Charlie. Note the sign.*

Later that summer, Charlie gave me a scare. He had come to stay in the cat room for ten days while Mark was out of town. One morning when I went out to feed him his breakfast, I found the tail half of my snake skin in the middle of the floor! I had completely forgotten that it was displayed on a wall shelf in that room. Charlie had found it, played with it, and, I feared, eaten the half with the head on it. I hunted everywhere, but I couldn't find the rest of the snake skin.

I was afraid Charlie would get sick. I watched him carefully all day, but he showed no signs of a stomachache. I threw the remaining half of the snake skin away. It wasn't nearly as interesting without the head.

When Mark came to take Charlie home, I told him what had happened.

"Yum, yum," Mark said. "Snake crunchies."

"Blah," I replied.

By then it was obvious that Charlie's little snack had not hurt him, so we were able to laugh about how Charlie must have had a fine old time batting that snake skin around, and then eating half of it.

I still miss Carl and always will, but his workshop is no longer a sad, empty space. It's now known as the cat room, complete with a HOME FOR WAYWARD CATS: STRAYS WELCOME sign that hangs on the outside of my house, with an arrow pointing to the cat room door.

Fourteen months after Carl died, the date marking our fiftieth wedding anniversary approached. I wanted to honor that day, so I arranged with Susan to have a private tour of Pasado's Safe Haven for my family.

Carl and I had been involved with the sanctuary from its beginning. We had attended court hearings for cruelty cases that the staff was involved in, and we were financial backers of their spay/neuter program for low-income pet owners.

I'd been to the sanctuary many times, including once when Carl donated two dozen of his hand-crafted birdhouses for the sanctuary gift shop to sell, but my kids and grandkids had never been there.

It was the perfect way to spend my special day. We met many rescued animals, including Louise, the pig that I wrote about in *Trapped*. We saw the dog barn that Carl and I had given in Daisy's memory, and the lovely bird feeding area that our friends Larry and Myra Karp had donated to honor Carl and me. I rested on a garden bench, donated by Judi and Greg Farrar in memory of Carl. Greg took the photographs for *Shelter Dogs: Amazing Stories of Adopted Strays*.

We laughed when a goose tried to peck Pam, my daughter-in-law. The kids fed carrots to the donkey, played with the dogs, and petted a llama. Best of all, when we got to Kitty City, Mama came to greet us. I like to think she remembered me. She rubbed on my ankles and purred while I stroked her fur. She flopped on her side for a tummy rub.

It was not the fiftieth anniversary that I had always anticipated, but it was a happy time, filled with family, good memories, and rescued animals. Fifty years after my wedding day, I was surrounded by love.

# I Bailed Him Out, and Then He Bit Me

*G*us showed up as a stray. I found him on my front porch, mooching Mr. Stray's food. Gus was a big boy whose tabby-striped fur had a lovely golden hue. His most distinguishing feature was his tail, which was short with a knobby twist on the end. Gus's tail looked as if someone had tied a knot in it when he was small, and the tail had stayed that way as it grew. I don't know if he was born with an odd tail or if his tail had been injured.

Right from the start, Gus rubbed against my ankles and purred when I petted him. Most strays are skinny, but Gus appeared to be well fed. He had no identification. I thought perhaps he was lost. Maybe his family had been moving and he jumped out of the car. Maybe he'd run away during a thunderstorm. I felt sure that someone would be looking for such a beautiful, friendly cat.

However he came to be in my yard, Gus made it clear that he intended to stay. Why would he leave when there was ample free food on my porch?

Anne claims the cats have a secret signal posted on my fence, like the runaway slaves had back before emancipation, announcing that mine is a safe house where they'll be fed if they come to my door.

I was reluctant to move Gus into the cat room. Foster cats who come to me from an established rescue group, as Edgar did, have the benefit of the group's web site, adoption events, and networking efforts. Their pictures get posted online and their good attributes are touted to prospective adopters. When I rescue a cat by myself, I have no one to help me find it a home. My friends all have their quota of pets and I knew if I brought Gus into the foster cat room, he could easily be there for several months before I found him a good home. I'd been incredibly lucky with Charlie, and it was not likely to happen again.

I couldn't ask Susan to take Gus because Pasado's accepts only rescued cats. Mama had qualified because of the pellet gun, and the kittens. Gus was considered a stray, and Kitty City simply did not have the space or funds to take in strays.

I decided that this time I would take him to the Pierce County Humane Society. That's where Willie had been reunited with his family, so I knew the system sometimes worked. Gus was so friendly that I thought he might really be lost, and if that were the case, his people would look for him at the shelter. That's why we have such an agency, I told myself—to reunite lost pets with their owners, and to care for strays and find them good homes.

I put Gus in the carrier, drove him to the Humane Society, and turned him over to them. People who relinquish animals are asked to make a donation. I gave them one hundred dollars.

Then I drove home, and began to worry. This Humane Society is a good facility, one that was working toward being a no-kill shelter. As a donor, I received their reports. I knew they had met their goal of not euthanizing any healthy, adoptable dogs the year before—but they had not yet managed to achieve that with cats. They kept the cats as long as possible, but if they were not adopted, eventually they were euthanized to make room for the next batch of homeless cats.

What if nobody was looking for Gus? Maybe he wasn't lost. Perhaps he had been dumped.

Being at the shelter was better than being on his own, but I wondered what Gus's chances were of being adopted. There are many more people at the shelter looking for a cute little kitten than there are folks who want an adult cat of unknown age and background. I remembered what had happened with Mama.

When I looked at the Humane Society's web page, I panicked. They currently had seventy-six cats available for adoption. Seventy-six! It was highly unlikely that all seventy-six of those cats would find permanent loving homes. What if Gus didn't get chosen? I thought about how friendly Gus was, how he purred when I petted him. He would make a wonderful house cat for someone, but who would advocate for him when he was one of seventy-six?

The next afternoon I returned to the Humane Society. I reasoned that if Gus's owners had been looking for him, they would have found him within a day of his arrival at the shelter.

When I got there, I saw Gus lying in a cage, one in a long row of cages, waiting for someone to adopt him. The cage was clean, and he had food, but he lay there listlessly, as if he had no hope.

When I tapped on the glass, Gus looked at me, then stood up and butted his head against the glass. I was sure he recognized me and wanted me to pet him, but we were separated by the glass wall on his cage. I couldn't stand it. I told the cat room attendant my name and said I had brought Gus in the day before. "I've changed my mind," I said. "I want to take him back."

"I'm sorry," she said. "We can't return him. Once an animal has been turned over to the agency, the only way to get it back is to officially adopt it."

*Gus, waiting to be adopted*

She brought me the papers to fill out, including the one where I agreed to pay the sixty-five-dollar adoption fee. I mentioned that I had made a one-hundred-dollar contribution the day before when I brought Gus in.

"I'm sorry," she said again. "Contributions are nonre-turnable."

I filled out all the paperwork, paid the sixty-five-dollar adoption fee, and made Gus officially my cat. Gus had not been neutered and, since the adoption fee included neutering, I left him overnight to have the surgery done. I figured, I might as well save the cost of having my own vet neuter him, and Gus would be spared an extra car ride and being left at the veterinary clinic.

The next day I drove to the Humane Society again, and that time I put Gus back in the carrier and took him home with me. As soon as I let him out of the carrier in the cat room, he began to explore. One workbench is under a window that has a view of a bird feeder. Edgar used to like to sit there and watch the birds, so when I noticed two blue jays at the feeder, I lifted Gus up on the workbench, thinking he would like to watch the birds, too. Instead, he immediately turned and started to jump down.

Since he had just been neutered, I was afraid the long jump onto the hard concrete floor might hurt him. I grabbed for him, to lift him down, and when Gus saw my hands mov-ing suddenly toward him, he bit me.

Blood trickled down the side of my hand. His teeth had made several deep punctures. I knew that cat bites can easily get infected, so I thoroughly washed my hand right away and put some disinfectant on it. When I returned to the cat room with a bandage on my hand, Gus hurried to greet me, purring and pushing his head against my ankles. I knew he had bitten me only because he was nervous after his shelter ordeal and a car ride. He had gone through a lot of trauma in a short time, found himself in yet another strange place, and my sudden movement had startled him. He was not a vicious animal, and I was not afraid to pet him or even to pick him up.

"It's all right," I told him as he snuggled on my lap. "I know you didn't mean to hurt me." He sniffed at my bandage, and kneaded his claws in and out on my jeans.

Before I went to bed I put more disinfectant on the place where Gus had bit me. I awoke in the night with my hand throbbing. The pain extended all the way up my arm past my elbow, and I was sure that the bite was infected. Pain pills helped me make it to daylight, but I couldn't sleep.

The next day was Sunday; my doctor's office was closed. I knew I couldn't wait until Monday for medical treatment, so I went to the emergency room of the hospital. The doctor there confirmed my diagnosis of infection and started me on antibiotics. I also had to get a tetanus shot, since it had been many years since I'd had one. He warned me that a cat bite can be serious and told me to have my own doctor check the bite again in two days.

It took three doctor visits and two rounds of strong

antibiotics to finally get rid of the infection. I added my medical costs to what I'd paid the Humane Society, and wondered if the Guinness World Records folks had a category for Most Expensive Stray Cat.

While my hand healed, I became more and more fond of Gus. His laid-back personality made him an easy cat to love. He was a happy boy who purred at everything and everyone. He never tried to sneak outside or even to come in the house with me. He was always glad to see me, but he seemed perfectly content to stay in the cat room. He liked it when I dangled the feather toy for him, or tossed a catnip mouse, but he was also happy to sit on his blanket and meditate. Mostly, he wanted to be petted.

As I watched Gus's acceptance of whatever came his way, and the quiet pleasure he found in his simple life, I decided the world would be a better place if a few more people behaved like Gus.

I wanted to keep Gus but I reminded myself that I had wanted to keep Edgar, too, and no doubt would have wanted to keep Charlie if he'd been here longer. My goal was to give the rescued cats the love and care that they needed until they went into their permanent homes.

As I had done with Edgar, I printed some flyers. I put a picture of Gus on them, over the words GUS NEEDS A HOME.

Under that was a brief description of all his good qualities, along with my name and e-mail address.

He'd had his first vaccinations at the Humane Society but when he needed a booster shot a month later, I took him to my own vet, where he charmed everyone at the clinic. I asked if I could post one of my flyers, and they not only agreed to take it, but said they would keep it on the front counter where all of their clients would see it.

The person who cuts my hair is an animal lover, and she agreed to post Gus's flyer in her hair salon. The small independent bookstore that I frequented put Gus's flyer up. I even took one to the assisted-living facility where Chester lived, and made a pitch for how calm Gus was and how he'd be a great cat for an elderly person.

Nobody contacted me about adopting Gus. Nothing happened for four months. Then one day I had an e-mail from someone named Jackie who was interested in learning more about Gus. She gave me her phone number. I called her immediately and discovered that she had seen my flyer at my vets' office and recognized my name.

"You are my granddaughter's favorite author," she told me. "Emma is ten, and she loves your books. She's told me that you rescue animals, but I never thought I'd be able to help you with one of them."

We talked awhile and I felt certain that Jackie would give Gus a good home, if she decided to take him. We set a time for her to come out the next day to meet Gus.

I called the vet's office to tell them what had happened. They were not surprised.

"She got so excited when she saw that flyer," the girl at the desk told me. "She took out her cell phone right then and called her daughter and said, 'We can't let a cat of Peg Kehret's go without a home.'"

I couldn't believe it. Author recognition was going to help me find a home for Gus! The vet also told me that Jackie had been a client for many years, took wonderful care of her animals, but had no pets at that time. The day she saw the flyer, she'd been there to pick up her daughter's dog.

Jackie arrived with a cat carrier and fell in love with Gus immediately. Who wouldn't? By then he was a big old purr factory. He went straight to Jackie and rubbed against her ankles. *Atta boy, Gus,* I thought. *Turn on the charm, big guy.*

Jackie and I hit it off right away, and even discovered that we had mutual friends.

I told Jackie about the bite but it didn't worry her.

"Given those circumstances, I don't blame him," she said.

There was never one second of doubt that Gus was going home that day with Jackie.

I was thrilled that Gus had found such a perfect family, but I still wept when Jackie's car left my driveway with Gus inside.

"Have a good life, Gus," I whispered. "I'm going to miss you."

I invited Jackie to bring Emma, her granddaughter, out to my house, which she did a week or so later. They also came when I gave a talk at one of the local libraries, and Jackie has been wonderful about e-mailing me periodic reports with the subject line: Gus the Magnificent.

When Gus had lived with her for a year, Jackie told me she'd taken him to the vet for a checkup and that he'd been put on a diet.

"The good life caught up with him," she said. "He weighs more than sixteen pounds."

Since he had weighed twelve and a half pounds when he left here, and I thought he was big then, a diet sounded like a reasonable suggestion.

Gus taught me that even a mild-mannered and loving animal will sometimes bite if it feels threatened. I also learned that I need to do the best I can to help every animal, even when I'm tired and it isn't convenient, even when I know I'm making a commitment that could possibly last for several months.

I wish I had never taken Gus to the Humane Society. It

felt wrong for me to leave him there when I had an alterna-
tive—my own cat room—and it felt right when I went back
and bailed him out. I should have listened to my inner voice
and kept Gus here from the start, trusting that eventually I
would find the perfect home for him, which is exactly what
happened.

# Short Stays

After Gus left, there was a stretch of time where I had several rescues but the animals stayed with me for only a short time. It began when I drove down my driveway one afternoon and found a pony standing on the other side of the gate. I opened the gate and looked both ways to see if someone was with him. I didn't see a person, but I did see another pony!

Neither animal had on a halter or a saddle or any other equipment. The street that goes by my house is a private road and doesn't get much traffic, but it's only about a mile to the curvy two-lane highway that leads to Mt. Rainier National Park. Cars often drive too fast there, especially those going downhill. I certainly wouldn't want a loose pony on that stretch of road.

There's also some vacant land not far from my property, where a narrow path leads back to the old railroad bed trail and the acres of forest on the other side of that. If the ponies followed that path, they could easily be miles away in a short time.

I decided the best thing would be to coax them to come through my gate and then shut them in while I tried to find out where they belonged. They'd be safe on my property until I could find their owner.

The ponies seemed wary of my car, so I parked it out on the road. I returned to the house, got a bag of carrots, and walked back down the driveway. The ponies were grazing on the grass between my fence and the road. Leaving the gate open, I stood inside it, held up the carrots, and called to them. To my relief, they both ambled over to me. I tossed the carrots a few feet down the driveway, and, as they hurried toward the treats, I closed the gate.

I got in the car and drove about a mile to a house where I remembered seeing small horses, or perhaps they'd been ponies, in an open corral. Nobody was home. I noticed that the gate of the corral was standing open and there wasn't any animal inside it or nearby. I wrote down the address, went home, looked at the county records online to find the owner of that property, and got a phone number.

The homeowner recognized his ponies from my description, but he was at work and said it would take over an hour for him to get home. Meanwhile, the ponies had made their way around my house and were chomping on the grass in my backyard. I watched one pony take a drink from the birdbath.

When I was ten, my parents had friends whose daughter had a pony named Merrylegs. When we visited them, I sometimes got to ride it. I adored Merrylegs and dreamed of having a pony of my own. For a few brief hours, my dream had come true, and I was sorry when the grateful owner showed up to claim his animals.

The next short-term visitor was an elderly dachshund that I picked up when I was on my way to get a flu shot. The flu vaccine was scarce that year. Because I have a compromised immune system, as well as a history of getting the flu, I always get a flu shot. That year I had been unable to get one because none of the usual providers, including my doctor, received their supply of vaccine.

The day of the dachshund, Anne had called. "The University of Washington Health Clinic has flu vaccine," she told me. "They're giving the shots to anyone in the high-risk category, but you have to be over there before three o'clock. If you come to my house, I can drive you over and drop you off so you don't have to park and walk."

"I'll leave right now," I said, and I did.

I was barely out of my driveway, when I saw a miniature dachshund walking slowly along the side of the road, as if it were in pain. Because the dog's muzzle was gray, I knew it was an elderly animal. From the way she moved, I wondered if she'd been hit by a car. She wore no collar.

I pulled over and called the dog, but she ignored me. I suspected she was deaf. I went to her, let her sniff my fingers, and gingerly picked her up. I feared I would hurt her even more by handling her, but I couldn't leave her plodding along the road. She didn't struggle, and I put her in the car and drove off.

My plan was to stop at my vet's office, explain why I couldn't stay with the dog, ask them to examine her and keep her until I returned, probably about five o'clock. I was sure they'd be glad to do this, and it was only about a mile out of my way to go there. Maybe the dog was microchipped, and the vet could call the owner.

I pulled up in front of the clinic. It was dark inside. I tried the door. It was locked. There wasn't any sign saying "back in ten minutes" or some such. I could not imagine why the clinic was closed in the middle of a weekday. Nonetheless, nobody was there.

I couldn't take an elderly, possibly injured dog to Seattle with me to the University Health Clinic, so I called Anne.

"I'm bringing a rescued dog with me," I said.

"Why am I not surprised?" she replied.

I told her what had happened, and asked her to call her own vet and see if we could drop the dog there while we went to Seattle, and then come back for her. If not, we'd have to shut the dachshund in a room at Anne's house, which I knew would upset her dog, Otter.

Anne's vet agreed to my plan, so we dropped the dachshund off and drove to Seattle. I made it to the clinic with five minutes to spare, and got my flu shot. Then we returned to Anne's vet, who said there wasn't anything wrong with the dachshund except old age. She had no injuries; she just had arthritis.

I took the dog home with me but instead of leaving her in the workshop, I put her in the bathroom that adjoins my bedroom. Because of the cabin's radiant heat, the floors are always warm, and I felt the elderly dog would be more comfortable with the heated floor to soothe her arthritic joints.

I gave her a soft blanket and, unlike Willie, she made a

nest and settled on top of it. I gave her some of Lucy's food and a bowl of water.

Then I started making phone calls to all the people who lived in my area. Some were home, but they didn't know of anyone who had a dachshund. Some calls resulted in voice mail, and I left messages describing the dog and giving my phone number.

Before I went to bed that night, I put one of Lucy's leashes on the dachshund and took her outside. I left Lucy in, because I didn't want an excited Lucy to bother the elderly dog. Watching me out there with another dog, Lucy scratched at the glass door and howled. When the dachshund paid no attention, I knew she was deaf.

Lucy also had a hard time settling down to go to sleep that night because she knew the dachshund was in the bathroom. Molly, as usual, was furious that I had brought yet another animal home. She sat outside the bathroom, perfecting her scowl. The dachshund didn't help matters any by snuffling and making noises all night long. I didn't get much sleep.

About ten o'clock the next morning, my phone rang. It was Heidi, a woman who lives near the pony owner. I didn't see her often, but I always enjoyed talking to her.

"You have Hannah!" she said.

"The dachshund?" I said.

"Yes, she's mine. I've had her since I was in high school."

"I never saw her when I was at your house," I said.

"I always shut her in the bedroom when anyone comes. She's completely deaf and nearly blind. I worry that she'll wander out when someone opens the door, and then get hit by a car in the driveway. I have no idea how she got loose yesterday. She sleeps most of the time now, so I didn't miss her when I got home. I had to work late last night and didn't see your message until this morning."

"She doesn't have any ID on," I said.

Heidi groaned. "She's always worn a collar and a tag. Always! I took it off the night before last when I gave her a bath. Then I washed the collar, too, and it wasn't dry yet when I left for work yesterday."

"So Hannah chose her one day without a collar to go exploring," I said. We both laughed.

Heidi came to retrieve old Hannah, and stayed to visit awhile. We discovered a mutual love of animals that has become a strong friendship in the years since. She eventually took animal rescue and veterinary technician training, and is a team leader with the Washington State Animal Rescue Team, which aids animals during disasters such as floods. In *Ghost Dog Secrets*, I named the animal control officer Heidi in her honor.

I called my vet's office because I was concerned about why the clinic had been closed. I learned they'd canceled all afternoon appointments that day in order to attend the funeral of the mother of one of the staff members. They'd put a message on their answering machine, but not on the door.

Not long after Hannah's sleepover at my house, an acquaintance, Diane, who also does foster care for animals, called one morning, nearly in tears. "One of my neighbors found two tiny kittens in their shrubs," she said. "There's been no sign of the mother cat, and the two kittens are only about three weeks old. They need to be bottle-fed."

I knew she had fostered very young kittens in the past, so I said, "Are you taking care of them?"

"I can't!" she wailed. "I've had little kittens for the past three weeks and have had to get up in the night with them every night. They left yesterday and Scott [her husband] says NO MORE. He's sick of having his sleep interrupted every night. If I take another batch of kittens so soon, I'm afraid he'll move out."

I realized where this conversation was going.

"I know it's a lot to ask," she said, "but I don't know who else to call."

"I've never taken care of kittens that young," I said.

"I'll show you what to do," she said. "I can bring the

bottles and the kitten formula. Please, please take them. Scott will have a fit if they're still here when he gets home."

What could I do? She was there an hour later. Because they each fit easily in the palm of my hand, I called them Teeny and Tiny.

Instead of putting them in the cat room, I put them in my front bathroom. There was enough space for a litter box, a small scratching post, and a cat bed. The floor would keep them warm and, best of all, the bathroom had no hiding places for kittens.

*Me holding Teeny and Tiny*

Diane showed me how to mix the formula and told me how much to give them. They nursed happily on the bottles and seemed to like being held. They needed to be fed every three hours, around the clock, but lack of sleep wasn't my big problem. The real difficulty, as always, was how to find someone who wanted to adopt them.

I called all my friends, in case someone had miraculously decided they wanted to adopt a cat since the last time I talked to them. No such luck.

My granddaughter Brett came to visit and took over the kitten feeding for a day. She wanted to keep them, of course, but her dad is allergic to cats and she would be graduating from high school soon and going away to college.

Teeny and Tiny grew quickly and were able to go a longer time in between feedings. Soon they started sleeping through the night, and I began giving them solid food.

I had told Heidi, Hannah the dachshund's person, about the kittens. She called me shortly after the kittens were weaned.

"I think I have a home for the kittens," she said.

"Kittens, plural?" I said. "Someone wants both of them?"

"Yep. A guy I work with has been wanting a cat, and he says he'll take them both so they can keep each other company. I've known him for years; he'll give them a good home."

"You can quit sulking," I told Molly. "They're leaving tonight."

There was a satisfying justice in the way this had worked out. I had helped Heidi when her dog was lost, and now she helped me when I had kittens who needed a home.

Teeny and Tiny were only with me a little over two weeks and they had already found a home where they could stay together forever. I wish all cats who need homes would be adopted so quickly.

# The Poacher

One night I was awakened by Lucy growling. I got up to investigate and, as I walked from my bedroom to the living room, I heard a loud *thunk!* on my back porch. I switched on the outside lights and found myself inches away from a large black bear! He stood on the other side of the glass door, apparently as surprised to see me as I was to see him.

The thunk I'd heard was my large cedar bin, where I keep sunflower seeds for the bird feeder, falling over. He had been trying to open it, to get at the seeds. I pounded on the glass, but the bear didn't budge. I grabbed a big brass school bell—the Iowa Children's Choice Award, which is engraved with my name, *Nightmare Mountain*, and 2003—and rang it.

*The bear is standing at the entrance
to my nature trail.*

*Clang! Clang!* That set Lucy into a frenzy of barking, and the bear lumbered off the porch. I cracked open the door far enough to put my hand out and rang the bell some more. The bear hurried around the side of the house.

I looked out the front window and saw him eyeing the bird feeder there. Since he was in front, it seemed safe to go on the back porch, so I dragged the cedar bin into the living room. Then I looked out in front again. He was still there, pawing at the bird feeder. I stuck my hand out the front door and swung the bell back and forth several times. Off he went.

I continued to see the bear in my yard for the next two days and was able to take some pictures of him using the zoom feature on my camera.

I looked around carefully before I went outside.

I took down the bird feeders, kept Lucy on a leash, and only fed Mr. Stray when I saw him on the porch waiting for food because I was afraid cat food would attract the bear, just as the birdseed had.

Some of my friends urged me to contact the wildlife department and report the bear. "They'll come and trap him," I was told. "They can shoot him with a tranquilizer dart, and then relocate him."

I didn't want to do that. Unless the bear became aggressive and caused trouble, I didn't see any reason to take him away from his usual habitat. I didn't want him on my porch, or hanging around the house, but he was welcome to live in the woods.

After the third day, I didn't see the bear again. He was apparently only passing through. I replaced the bird feeders and put the bin of seed back on my porch.

Three years later, I looked out my office window late one afternoon and saw a black bear in my yard. By the time I had grabbed the school bell and hurried into the living room, he was already on my porch, trying to get the cedar bin open.

Was it the same bear, and he remembered the bin? Or did both bears simply smell the seeds and try to reach them? Bears have a much better sense of smell than humans do. They also tend to return to places where they've successfully found food in the past.

Black bears are solitary animals who roam large territories—as much as eighty square miles. I wondered if the birdseed bin on my porch was going to be a regular stop on the bear's route. If so, I'd have to find someplace else to store the sunflower seeds.

Without opening the door, I rang the brass bell, which made Lucy bark. The noise worked, and the bear hurried off, headed into the woods toward the public trail that adjoins my property on the back side.

Ten minutes later my phone rang. A man who lives about a mile away, whom I had met at neighborhood meetings, told me, "I just shot a bear on the trail. I wounded it, and it climbed over your fence into your property." He was calling to ask permission to come on my land to hunt for it.

My property is a wildlife sanctuary. It is posted No Hunting. Under ordinary circumstances, I would never give anyone permission to hunt here. That day, my big concern was for the bear. If he was wounded, as this man said, I didn't want him to suffer and die a lingering death in my woods.

I also worried that a wounded bear could be dangerous. I

was flying to Indiana the next morning to receive the Young Hoosier Book Award, and I didn't want my pet sitter, Karrie, to have to deal with a wounded bear. So I reluctantly said yes, and the hunter began his search.

I hung up the phone and agonized over my decision. I hadn't wanted the bear on my porch, but I didn't want him dead, either, and I especially hated the idea of having him stalked and killed on my property, where I'd always said all animals are welcome. If I had known then what I learned later, I would not have given permission, but I did what I thought was best at the time.

Only twenty minutes later, it got dark, and the hunter came to tell me the hunt was called off for the night. He said he'd be back first thing in the morning. I felt sick to my stomach all night long. Allowing someone to hunt here went against my basic beliefs, yet I worried about the bear's suffering, and about Karrie and Lucy and Mr. Stray. A black bear's diet is mainly grasses, roots, insects, and berries, but I knew they would also eat fish and mammals, if that's what was available. Would a wounded bear attack a cat or a small dog?

I had to leave for the airport at seven fifteen the next morning. The hunter's car was parked on my driveway, and I knew he was already there, searching for the bear in my woods. I nearly canceled my trip but I didn't want to disappoint the Indiana librarians, and I knew my presence at home was not going to affect the outcome of the bear hunt, so I drove to the airport in a state of anxiety.

I had taken the hunter's name and cell phone number the night before, and I called him before I boarded my plane. By then he had spent three hours combing every inch of my land. He said he'd brought his dog, who repeatedly picked up the scent and always followed it to the same place in my fence. The bear had apparently been able to climb back over the fence and escape into the woods in the valley below my property. When I heard that, I realized I had been wrong to allow the hunter to pursue the bear on my land. Clearly the bear was able to get around. His wounds might heal. He might still be okay.

As soon as I got home from Indiana, I began studying bears. One of the most interesting things I learned was that animals who are wounded by hunters will often heal on their own if they are left to do so. That knowledge gave me hope that my bear had not only escaped, but survived. However, it also filled me with guilt and horror that I had given permission for someone to come on my land and try to kill the bear. What if the hunter had seen it that first night? What if his dog had treed it the next morning? The bear would have been dead, and I would have been responsible. Black bears in the wild have an average life span of twenty years. I had no idea how old this bear was, but he had no obvious health problems. Perhaps he had many more years to live.

I also learned about hunting regulations and discovered that besides being illegal to hunt anything on the public trail, where this bear had been shot, there is no bear season at all where I live. So the hunter was a poacher, who hunted illegally and shot a protected animal.

Bears are the most intelligent native animals in North America. They are rarely aggressive toward humans, the one exception being a mother bear protecting her cubs. I knew this bear had not attacked the hunter. It had run away from me the minute I made noise, and the hunter admitted that he shot the bear as soon as he saw it, without waiting to see what the bear would do.

Years earlier, I had written *The Hideout*, a book about bear poaching. During the research for that book I learned that poachers often shoot bears and other animals inside our national parks. This had made me furious, and now a poacher who was trying to illegally kill animals right in my own neighborhood made me angrier. Even worse, I had temporarily gone along with the misinformed notion that a wounded bear must be killed.

Education is a powerful tool. Once I knew that hunting

is not legal on this trail and that bears in my county are a protected species, I was prepared to take a stand if I ever saw the poacher again. Animals cannot speak for themselves; sometimes we have to do it for them.

Two weeks passed with no sign of the bear. Then one morning I found both of my bird feeders on the ground. They had been ripped off the poles that they are nailed to, and I knew only a bear would be strong enough to do that. The next night, a suet feeder that had hung on a fence was torn down, and the suet was gone. I rejoiced to find this destruction because I was certain it meant that the bear had survived.

The third night I left the outdoor lights on and stayed in my recliner instead of going to bed, hoping to see the bear. I was curious to see if he showed any signs of his injury. Did he walk with a limp? Could he use both front paws normally? All night long, I peeked out the window, waiting and watching.

He didn't show up that night. I wondered if the lights made him nervous, so the next night I left the lights off. Every ten or fifteen minutes, I'd click them on but again I saw no bear. He has not been back since. By then it was late November, so I assume that his scavenging for birdseed had been part of his effort to fatten up before winter.

Black bears are dormant in their dens in the wintertime.

They don't eat or drink, but live off the fat they've stored in their bodies. They eat as much as they can in the summer and fall, preparing for their dormant season.

I often see news stories about bear sightings in the suburbs. Usually the bear is shot with a tranquilizer gun and relocated, but sometimes they are killed. A recent news story told of an eleven-year-old boy who saw a bear in his yard and, fearing it would "hurt his sisters," he got a gun and killed it. The report saddened me, both for the bear, who had done nothing aggressive, and for the child who now knows what it is like to kill a living creature.

Ever since the poacher incident, I've felt protective of bears, especially any who might live in my area. When the first bear was here for a few days several years ago, I didn't call the wildlife department, and that turned out to be the right decision, as the bear moved on without hurting anything.

I made the wrong decision for the second bear (or maybe it was the same bear on his second visit) mainly because I was ignorant of the ways of black bears. I've learned about bears since then, and I've also learned more about myself. It is always wrong to take an action that goes against my core beliefs. I should have said no to the poacher when he asked to hunt on my property. If I was concerned about Karrie, I could have canceled my trip and stayed home. If I feared that the bear was suffering, I could have asked a trusted friend who respects wildlife to walk my woods with his gun, knowing he would have shot the bear only to end its suffering if it was dying anyway. Even though the bear was hurt, he deserved a chance to get away and to live longer. I'm glad he got that opportunity.

Two weeks after the bear poacher incident, in the last hour of the last day of that year's deer hunting season, the same poacher shot a beautiful blacktail deer. Once again, he was hunting on the public trail. Once again, he wounded but did not kill the animal, and it ran on to private property. This time it was a vacant lot, one that was posted NO HUNTING. The poacher followed the wounded deer and killed it. I heard the shots.

My closest neighbor, whose property is between me and the vacant lot and who shares my love for wildlife, saw the whole incident and called to tell me what had happened. "It's the same guy who shot the bear," he said.

This time, I knew that hunting on the trail wasn't legal. Neither was shooting an animal on private property without permission, which is what the poacher had done. I dialed 911 and reported the poacher. It was late on a Sunday afternoon. I live in an unincorporated part of the county, where law enforcement officials such as game wardens cover hundreds of miles of territory. I knew it was unlikely that anyone would arrive in time to catch the poacher.

I don't know if an official responded to my call or not. If they did, they got there after dark, long after the poacher had gutted the deer and hauled the carcass away.

It didn't seem right to let the poacher get away with his illegal hunting. On Monday morning I called the state Fish and Wildlife Department and reported both poaching incidents, the bear and the buck. The person I talked to was horrified that anyone would shoot a bear in this jurisdiction, and was equally dismayed to learn that both shootings had happened on the public trail.

"Even during a lawful deer season," he said, "it is not legal to hunt on the trail. Families hike there. People ride their horses and walk their dogs."

"I know," I replied. "I walk my dog there myself."

I knew the poacher's name because he'd given me his name and phone number the night he shot the bear. When the wildlife officer asked if I knew who the poacher was, I had no qualms about passing along that information. He promised to send an enforcement officer to the poacher's home to speak with, and possibly cite, him.

Two friends felt I should not have reported the poacher, for fear that he would retaliate, but if I had not turned him in, the illegal hunting would surely have continued. As far as I am aware, there has been no more hunting on the trail.

The bear has not returned, but whenever I open the cedar bin on my porch to get sunflower seeds for my bird feeders, I look at the teeth marks that remain on one corner of the lid, and I hope he is safe, and well.

# Throwaway Cat

Much to Molly's delight, I had a few weeks without any rescued animals.

I was hard at work on the revisions of *Ghost Dog Secrets*, and I wanted to concentrate on my writing for a while before I offered to take another foster cat.

Then my friend Jenny called one morning to tell me that she'd seen a car driving slowly past her house. Curious, she had watched out the window and was shocked when she saw the driver stop the car, get out, open the back door, shove a cat into the street, and drive off!

"I ran out and yelled at him," Jenny said, "but he sped away. I couldn't get a license number, or I would have reported him to the police. I think it's illegal to dump an animal."

"It is," I said, "but that doesn't stop people from doing it."

Jenny had managed to catch the frightened cat, and had put it in a cage in her yard. Her husband was in the VA hospital that week, and she drove to Seattle every day to be with him. There was no way she could deal with a rescued cat, so she called me. I assured her that I would pick up the cat, take it to my vet to be examined, and bring it home.

That turned out to be easier said than done.

I called my vet's office, told them I was picking up a rescued cat, and asked if I could bring her in for an exam on my way home. That way, we'd get started on any needed treatment right away. They agreed to see her. Jenny's house is a twenty-minute drive and by the time I got there, she had left for the hospital. The caged cat was in her backyard, with three pink roses lying on top of the cage. Jenny knows I love roses and had picked me a thank-you bouquet.

The cat, a beautiful fluffy-haired calico with the longest tail I've ever seen on a cat, meowed at me as I approached. I decided to call her Rosie, because of the flowers that adorned the cage.

I had brought my cat carrier and I set it on the ground next to the cage, so I could transfer her quickly. I opened the cage and reached inside for Rosie. She backed away, out of my reach.

"C'mon, kitty," I said. "I'm not going to hurt you." I

held my fingers toward her. She pressed herself against the rear of the cage and swished her tail nervously.

My arms were not long enough to reach her. I spent fifteen minutes trying to coax her to come out. When that didn't work, I lifted up the rear end of the cage until it was so high that Rosie had to move toward the end that was still on the grass. My plan was to reach in as soon as she got to the opening, grab her, and put her in the carrier.

Instead, when she was almost close enough for me to reach her, she suddenly bolted. I grabbed for her, and missed. Rosie flew out of the cage and raced around the corner of Jenny's house.

I rushed after her, but she had vanished. I scanned the yard, the street, the sidewalk, the yards across the street. There was no sign of a cat. I felt sick. How could I have let this happen? Poor Rosie!

Jenny has a thick honeysuckle bush on one corner of her property, between the lawn and the sidewalk. It's eight feet by four feet in size, with intertwined branches and leaves that form a thick, impenetrable mass. As I stood listening and looking for the cat, I heard movement from the depths of the honeysuckle.

I knelt on the grass and peered into the bush. I couldn't see her, but I heard movement again, and I was sure Rosie was hiding in the honeysuckle. Quickly, I retrieved the cat carrier from the backyard and positioned it beside the honeysuckle. I coaxed. I pleaded. I called. Rosie stayed in hiding.

Fifteen minutes passed. Half an hour. I knew I should call the vet but that number was not programmed into my cell phone, and I didn't dare leave the honeysuckle for fear Rosie would emerge and I wouldn't see her.

An hour passed. It was a hot day, and I grew thirsty.

My cell phone rang. It was the vet's office, wanting to know if I was still planning to bring the cat.

"I've run into a problem," I said, and explained what had happened. They told me if I could get the cat there before one o'clock, they could examine her but the vet was leaving then to do barn calls on horses all afternoon. I looked at my watch. It was eleven forty-five.

Because of my increased weakness from post-polio syndrome, I use a cane. I named the cane Alice, because it leads me into wonderland. My cane has cat faces all over it.

I considered poking Alice into the honeysuckle to nudge Rosie out but I was afraid when she got poked by the cane, she'd run and I wouldn't be able to catch her. At least when she was in the honeysuckle bush, she was safe and I knew where she was. I decided I needed help.

I saw a young woman weeding her garden about half

a block away. I walked over, keeping a nervous eye on the honeysuckle in case Rosie decided to emerge, and asked the woman if she would help me catch a cat who was hiding in the bushes. She looked a bit dubious, and I can't say that I blamed her.

I explained how the cat had been dumped out of a car and that I wanted to take it home and try to find someone to adopt it. "My name is Peg Kehret," I told her. "I'm a friend of Jenny and Jerry, who live in that house."

"Are you a writer?" she asked.

"Yes. I write books for kids."

Her wariness vanished. "My daughter loves your books," she said. "She'll be so excited when she comes home and finds out I helped you rescue a cat."

She followed me over to the honeysuckle bush. Once again, my books had brought me good luck with a cat rescue!

I poked Alice into the bushes, and we heard Rosie move. My new friend crouched on the ground, ready to grab Rosie. I poked again, and this time Rosie moved close enough that the woman could grasp one front leg. She held on until I could get a firm grip on Rosie, pull her through the honeysuckle, and put her in the carrier. Both of my arms were scratched from the honeysuckle branches, but Rosie was safe in the cat carrier.

The next day, I dropped off two autographed Pete the Cat books for my helper's daughter.

The vet said Rosie was healthy, so I made an appointment to have her spayed later that week. She moved in to the foster cat room, where she calmed down quickly and made herself at home. As always, my challenge was how to find someone to adopt her. Edgar had the benefit of belonging to Pasado's, so he could go to their official adopt-a-thon, and I'd been incredibly lucky with Charlie. I was on my own with Rosie, the same as I'd been with Gus.

Two days after Rosie got spayed, I noticed that her stomach was swollen and red where the stitches were. I took her back to the vet, who discovered that some of the suture material had broken inside, and Rosie had to have a second surgery to repair the damage. By the time she was fully healed and ready to be adopted, I'd already had her for a month.

I made flyers that said ROSIE NEEDS A HOME, added her picture, and posted them in all my usual places. Rosie had been with me three months before anyone expressed interest in her. The young woman who called told me she was new in the area and wanted a cat for company. She had seen my flyer when she accompanied a friend to pick up the friend's dog from a local veterinarian.

When she came to see Rosie, I asked if she'd ever had a pet before.

"I had two cats when I lived in California," she told me.

"What happened to them?"

"I gave them to my boyfriend when I moved, but he didn't keep them."

"Where are they now?"

She shrugged, clearly annoyed by my questions. "I don't know. What difference does it make?"

What difference does it make? Maybe what happened to her two cats didn't matter to her, but I was pretty sure it mattered to the cats, and her attitude made a difference to me. There was no way I'd let this young woman take Rosie. I told her I was interviewing more than one prospective adopter, and would let her know if I chose her.

"Forget it," she said. "I really don't want your cat anyway."

I held Rosie as I watched the car drive away. "We can do better than that," I told her. "You are not leaving until you go home with someone who will love you and take care of you for the rest of your life."

I've never understood how people can think of their pets as disposable. They wouldn't give away a child because they were moving. How can they give away a cat or a dog? Yet it happens all the time.

One morning I was sweeping the floor in Rosie's room when I stopped, staring in astonishment. I went straight to the phone and called Mark Smithberg.

"You'll never guess what Rosie did," I said.

"What?"

"She found the other half of the snake skin! Charlie didn't eat it after all."

I can not imagine where that snake skin was in the months between when Charlie played with it and when Rosie also decided it was a cat toy. Gus had occupied the room for four months, during which time I vacuumed often and fished balls and catnip mice out from under the workbench daily. I always clean thoroughly in between cats, and I had done that when Charlie went home the second time, after what Mark called "his vacation at Grandma's house." I cleaned extensively again when Gus got adopted. Where had the snake skin been all that time?

I don't know where Rosie found the snake skin, but she seemed disappointed when I deposited it in the garbage can.

Jenny called one afternoon and said, "I have someone who might be interested in Rosie." A former neighbor had dropped in to say hello. The woman lived alone but had always had a cat, so Jenny had asked, "How is your cat?"

The woman told her that the cat had died recently, at age

seventeen. "I miss her terribly," she said. "It's about time for me to get another cat."

"I know of one who needs a home," Jenny said, and she handed her friend one of my ROSIE NEEDS A HOME flyers. When her friend was enthusiastic, Jenny called me.

"When would she like to come and meet Rosie?" I asked.

"Are you busy right now?" Jenny asked. "I could come with her."

I put a couple of extra chairs in the cat room and brushed Rosie's fur. Half an hour later, Jenny and I watched as Carol petted Rosie, and Rosie rubbed against her. Rosie sat in Carol's lap and purred. Carol marveled at Rosie's long, gorgeous tail.

I showed her Rosie's medical records, which included all of her vaccinations, a rabies certificate, and the document showing she'd been spayed. I explained about the second surgery.

"You've spent a lot of money on her," Carol said, "but you're giving her to me."

"My hobby is rescuing cats," I said. "It's no more expensive than playing golf or shopping."

Carol borrowed Molly's carrier and took Rosie home with her that same day. When Jenny returned the carrier a week later, she reported that Rosie is queen of the household, a beloved companion who brings much joy to Carol.

Jenny had felt guilty about saving Rosie from a life on the street only to turn her over to me right away. It pleased us both that she was the one who found the perfect home for Rosie.

# Breaking My Own Rule

During most of the writing of this book, I had three pets—Lucy, Molly, and Mr. Stray. We rescued Molly at a campground in Indiana when she was six weeks old. Someone drove into the campsite across from ours, stayed five minutes, and left without their kitten. She finished our trip, and the rest of her life, with us. She lived seventeen and a half years.

For the final two years of her life, Molly had chronic renal failure, a kidney disease that is common in older cats. She lost a lot of weight and at one point, I didn't think she had long to live. For a month, I mixed warm water into her favorite kitty-num-num and offered it to her several times a day where she slept. Kitty Room Service helped, and Molly improved.

She grew frail, but she rolled on the bathroom rug every morning, begging for a tummy rub. On warm days, she liked to be outside for Kitty Meditation Hour. I stayed with her, to be sure she was safe. She always ate some grass, then waited until we were back inside to vomit it up. In her last months, she ate kitty-num-num exclusively and remained adamantly opposed to having any new cats in the house. I honored her wishes.

Two months after losing Molly, I offered to take a foster cat from the Seattle/King County Humane Society. I met with Katreva, the foster cat coordinator, who asked if I'd be willing to take Mia, age thirteen, who had been surrendered to the shelter six months earlier. The first foster family who took Mia returned her for urinating outside the litter box.

I remembered that as Molly got older, she sometimes stood too close to the side of the litter box and urinated over the edge. I had solved the problem by covering thin sheets of wood with foil and sticking them in the litter to make tall edges on three sides of the box.

I decided Mia deserved a second chance, so I brought her home. It's a ninety-minute drive. Mia complained loudly and peed in the carrier, but as soon as I opened the carrier in the cat room, she began to purr.

Her coat looked dull so I decided to brush her. I discovered that her rear end was dirty, with clumps of dried feces hanging in the fur. As I held her still with one hand and tried to clean her with wet paper towels, she bit me, breaking the skin on my thumb. It wasn't a deep bite but it drew blood. Remembering the terrible infection I got after Gus bit me, I doused my thumb with antiseptic, took extra vitamin C, and decided Mia would have to stay dirty until I had someone to hold her while I cleaned her filthy fur.

If I had not known that Mia was spayed, I would have thought she was about to deliver kittens. Her belly appeared bloated, giving her a pear shape. She loved to be petted, but not on her big stomach, and I noticed she eased her bulk down slowly when she lay down. When I had tried to clean her, I'd held her tightly around her stomach, which is probably why she nipped me.

I noticed, too, that she drank a lot of water and urinated more than is normal. Then I found tapeworm segments in the dried feces. I made an appointment to take her back to the Humane Society for a veterinary check.

When I e-mailed to make the vet appointment, I made the mistake of saying that Mia had bitten me. This required filing a bite report and going on a ten-day rabies watch. During that time, Mia would be taken off the website, which showcased adoptable cats. I knew Mia was not a vicious cat; there had been a good reason why she nipped me, but I filled out the report and turned it in. By the time the report was filed, the bite was completely healed with no problems.

Heidi came to help me clean Mia. She took one look at Mia's dirty rear end and announced, "Cat burrito!" She wrapped Mia tightly in a towel, with only her eyes and nose uncovered. My job was to hold Mia's head still while Heidi used her clippers to shave the fur under Mia's tail.

Wrapped like a burrito, Mia screeched her displeasure while I held on as hard as I could. It didn't take long, and Mia forgave us as soon as we let her loose.

On the day of her vet appointment, the long drive to the shelter was just as bad as it had been when I brought Mia home, only this time we had to go both directions on the same day. She peed in the carrier on the way in and pooped on the way home. She yowled the whole time. I felt terrible to put her through such an ordeal but I knew she needed medical care.

I was disappointed when I was not allowed to accompany her to be examined. I had made a list of my concerns, so I gave that to Katreva, to show to the vet.

Half an hour later, Mia and I were back in the car with a case of diet cat food. She had been wormed. The vet had drawn blood and would let me know the results of the blood tests. Someone mentioned that an X-ray of Mia's stomach might be useful, but the Humane Society clinic does not have an X-ray machine.

Mia and I were both exhausted when we finally got home, and I vowed I would not put her through the stress of that long trip again.

The blood tests showed some abnormalities. The most likely cause was feline infectious peritonitis (FIP), which is fatal to cats. I asked about the results of a urine test and was surprised to learn that no urine test had been done. They wanted to recheck Mia in a month.

The ten-days rabies watch had now ended, but Mia would stay off the adoptable list because of her health issues. Katreva said I could return her to the shelter if I wanted to, but there was no way I would have done that. I made sure FIP is not contagious to dogs, then said I would continue to foster Mia.

I immediately went online and learned all I could about FIP, including the fact that there is not a specific diagnostic test. When I read that one symptom is an accumulation of fluid in the abdomen, I felt sure that this was Mia's problem.

She refused to eat the diet cat food and, given the results of her blood tests, I didn't think her big stomach was caused by obesity anyway, so I began feeding her good quality canned food, which she loved. Kitty-num-num to the rescue once again!

By the time Mia had been here three weeks, she seemed to feel much better. She greeted me, purring loudly, whenever I entered the cat room. When I dangled a cat toy near her, she responded. Since she'd had no medical treatment, I assumed her improved condition was due to a stress-free environment.

Her large tummy still bothered her, though. She didn't want me to brush her there, and she continued to ease herself down. She still drank way too much water, which made her urinate often. When she'd been here two months, I requested permission from the Humane Society to take her to my own vet, in order to avoid the long car ride.

I offered to pay the costs myself, but the Humane Society rules state that foster animals must be treated only at the shelter. While I understood the reason for that, I also knew it was not the best choice for Mia. Katreva suggested that I leave Mia at the shelter and they would arrange for an appointment with an outside vet who had more specialized equipment, but that would mean having Mia spend three or four days back at the shelter. I knew how much that would upset her.

I decided to break my own rule of never keeping a foster animal permanently. I applied to adopt Mia. We set a time for me to go in to talk to the adoption counselor, sign the paperwork, and get all of Mia's medical records. I made an appointment with my own veterinarian for the day after that.

On the day of my appointment with the adoption

counselor, my horoscope in the morning paper warned me to consider the financial consequences of what I planned to do that day. I laughed. This cat was thirteen years old; she had known health problems, and veterinary care is not cheap. It seemed highly likely that my horoscope that day was accurate.

As soon as the adoption papers were signed, I changed her name to Purrlie. Mia had never felt right for this cat, and she did not respond to it. Because of her wonderful ever-ready purr, Purrlie seemed exactly right.

*Purrlie in her cat bed,*
*shortly after I adopted her*

Along with all of her medical records, I was given the paperwork that had been filled in by the person who had surrendered her to the shelter. One question was where the cat lived—indoors, outdoors, or a combination. She had been kept outdoors, even though she had been declawed in front (something I would never do) and had no way to defend herself.

The question "Who was her veterinarian?" had been left blank. So had the question "What's the best thing about this cat?" and "What's her favorite toy or game?" No wonder she didn't know her name. It didn't seem as if anyone had ever cared about her.

The medical records from the Humane Society were impressive. I immediately saw why they had not done a urine test at her last checkup. They had already done two urine tests in the previous four months. Two weeks after coming to the shelter, she had been isolated because she had quit eating. A number of exams and tests at that time showed nothing wrong. When she was given tranquilizers, she began eating again. Clearly, this cat did not do well in stressful conditions. It explained why she had improved so much with me, even without medical help.

Purrlie had been with me for nine weeks when I signed the adoption papers. I was already fond of her, but I was unprepared for my excitement that afternoon. When Purrlie was a Humane Society foster cat, I felt compassion for her. Now that she was *my* cat, I loved her. I would care for her as well as I could for the rest of her life.

I adopted Purrlie on a Monday and took her to my own vet on Tuesday. She weighed thirteen pounds. Because my father was born on September thirteenth, my family always considered thirteen to be a lucky number. I decided at thirteen pounds and thirteen years old, Purrlie must be a lucky cat.

*Adoption day*

After reviewing all Purrlie's records and examining her, Dr. Wood said the bloated stomach was not an accumulation of fluid, and she did not think Purrlie had FIP. She said some of the test results might have been caused by extreme stress. My hopes began to rise.

Dr. Wood took two X-rays of Purrlie's stomach, one from the side and one from the top. Both showed what looked like a large tumor. A new worry! We discussed the possibility of surgery, and Dr. Wood said she'd like to have an ultrasound first, to know exactly what we were dealing with. She said it would avoid what she called "peek and shriek surgery," where she might open up the stomach to remove the tumor only to discover that the tumor was entwined in vital organs or that there was some other reason why it could not be taken out.

A radiologist would bring the ultrasound equipment to the clinic. Usually, I was told, it takes a week or two to set up an appointment. I gave permission to do this and said I'd be available anytime the radiologist could come.

Meanwhile, I was dealing with a health problem of my own. My dentist had been concerned about a growth in my mouth and referred me to an oral surgeon. The surgeon said the growth was in an unusual place, and not a typical size. He recommended removing it and having a biopsy done. Not being eager to have oral surgery, I asked what the risks were if I decided to wait a while. I was told that if the growth was cancerous, and I didn't remove it, the cancer could spread before I had any further symptoms.

My oral surgery was scheduled on Wednesday, the day after Purrlie's appointment with Dr. Wood. Late Tuesday afternoon Dr. Wood's office called to say the radiologist could do Purrlie's ultrasound on Thursday morning. "This Thursday?" I asked. "The day after tomorrow?"

Yes, Purrlie's ultrasound would be the morning after my surgery. Purrlie shouldn't eat after seven the night before, and should be at the clinic at eight A.M.

I knew I'd still be woozy and on pain pills Thursday morning and shouldn't drive. My neighbor Vicki agreed to help me out.

I awoke with a sore mouth, aching jaw, and no energy. I longed to stay in my bathrobe and read all day. Instead, I showered, dressed, and got the cat carrier ready to transport Purrlie to the clinic. She was hungry and being stuffed into the carrier did not improve her outlook. It's a good thing Vicki was there to help and to lift the carrier into her car.

While Purrlie was sedated, had her tummy shaved, had the ultrasound, and recovered from the anesthetic, I got the house ready for her to become a member of the family.

Until then I had kept Purrlie in my separate foster cat room. Although I visited her there often, I always felt bad leaving her out there alone, rather than letting her have the run of the house. I didn't want to make Lucy adjust to a new cat if that cat wasn't going to stay permanently. Now that Purrlie was officially mine, she could be a house cat.

I put a fresh litter box where Molly's used to be, brought the big cat tree back into the living room so Purrlie could be up high where she'd feel secure, and arranged a food station on top of the clothes dryer, where Lucy couldn't get at it.

Late that morning, Dr. Wood called with good news. Purrlie did not have a tumor after all! She had a thick layer of falciform fat in her abdomen. There's no treatment for this, but it also won't kill her. Purrlie will always have a huge tummy and probably won't ever want to be touched there, but it will not prevent her from living out a normal life span.

I had adopted Purrlie believing she had FIP, a fatal disease. The next day I was told she didn't have FIP but she did have a large tumor. Now I suddenly had a cat with no FIP, and no tumor, either. I could hardly believe it.

There was still the problem of excessive thirst and urination, which may indicate diabetes. We started antibiotics for a suspected respiratory infection, but Dr. Wood agreed we could wait a while to retest Purrlie's urine since the Humane Society had already done that twice. Right then both Purrlie and I needed a few weeks with no doctor visits.

I could hardly wait for Purrlie to become a true house cat and companion. However, Purrlie had other ideas, mainly because she didn't like Lucy. She must have had a problem with a dog sometime in the past. I had already let them see each other through the baby gate many times, so I didn't anticipate this difficulty.

Lucy didn't bark at Purrlie or chase her, but she was curious and kept trying to get a closer look. Whenever Lucy approached her, Purrlie growled. Since Purrlie outweighed

Lucy by three pounds, Lucy wisely heeded Purrlie's warnings and stayed out of reach.

That evening I carried Purrlie into the living room and put her on the cat tree. Lucy couldn't get to her there and Purrlie could see the entire living area as well as a bird feeder outside the window. Purrlie wanted no part of it. She hissed, hopped down, and scurried back to her own space.

The next day I carried her into my bedroom, which is closer to the cat room, and put her on my bed. Same result: she hissed and ran back to the cat room.

I remembered how relieved Purrlie had been to leave her cage at the shelter and find herself in my foster cat room, where it was quiet. She had been happy there for over two months; I could understand why she wasn't in any hurry to leave.

One reason I've always liked cats is their independent spirit. A dog adopted from a shelter after spending six months there would be so grateful he'd follow me around for the rest of his life. Not Purrlie.

I decided this transition was going to work only if I let Purrlie make the choice, so I simply left the door between the cat room and the rest of the house open and hoped she would gradually explore the house and feel comfortable there. Eventually she did.

Two weeks after her adoption, I took her back to the vet because of the excessive thirst. This time another urine test showed that Purrlie was borderline diabetic. She went on a special food for diabetic cats. Dr. Wood gave me lessons in how to give insulin injections. My pet sitter, Karrie, offered to go with me and learn, too, so that when I was away she could take care of Purrlie.

As I handed the pharmacist my credit card for the insulin, syringes, and urine test strips, I calculated what I'd already spent on X-rays, an ultrasound, prescription food, and antibiotics. The Seattle/King County Humane Society's adoption fee for cats three years or older is just twenty-five dollars. Even so, Purrlie had now passed Gus for the Most Expensive Stray Cat honors.

The shots were not as difficult as I anticipated and Purrlie didn't seem to mind them. They needed to be given twelve hours apart, which required schedule juggling some days, but it was manageable.

After a month on the insulin, Purrlie's symptoms were unchanged. More testing showed she was still borderline diabetic. Dr. Wood now suspected that Purrlie had Cushing's disease, which is rare in cats. I read the list of symptoms and Purrlie had all of them. We decided to stop the insulin for two weeks, during which I would test Purrlie's urine each day with strips that measured blood glucose. Her glucose remained negative, so we stopped the insulin injections permanently.

Unfortunately there is no good treatment for Cushing's disease, which is usually caused by a tumor on the pituitary or adrenal gland. Thirty percent of cats who have surgery to remove a tumor die during the operation. By now Purrlie was almost fourteen years old; I was not going to put her through surgery.

The only available medication was seldom effective, and Purrlie had just endured a full month of twice-a-day antibiotic pills. She was a master at eating the tuna, cheese, Pill Pocket, or whatever else I used to disguise the pill—and leaving the pill untouched. All my life I've pilled a cat by crouching over her and squeezing her tightly between my knees while I opened her mouth with one hand and stuck the pill down with the other. This didn't work because of Purrlie's tender tummy. Besides, any activity that requires getting down on the floor is now an ordeal for me because, due to my post-polio weakness, I can't get up again.

After discussing the options with Dr. Wood, I decided not to treat Purrlie at all. I hope that her peaceful life and good nutrition will keep her comfortable and happy for a long time. So far, it seems to be working. She spends most of her time in the house now, tolerates Lucy as long as Lucy doesn't get too close, and purrs loudly when she's petted. She watches the birds and squirrels and hangs around the kitchen when I cook.

Unwanted by her first owners, Purrlie waited at the Humane Society for six months, but nobody chose her. Then her multiple health problems caused her to be labeled *unadoptable*. Now she has a loving permanent home where she lives a cat's dream life. She is even a Cover Cat! Yes, Purrlie is the cat I'm holding in the photograph on this book's cover. She purred while our picture was taken.

# Many Surprises

Some people object to calling an animal friend a pet. They think the word is demeaning and encourage us to say "companion animal" instead. While the animals with whom I live are certainly my dear companions, I also refer to them as my pets. To me, it is a loving word that means I have chosen those animals to share my life and am committed to caring for them as long as they live.

With one exception, every pet I ever had was a rescued animal. The exception was George, the cairn mix who was the unplanned purchase that Carl didn't know about until after I did it.

I bought George at a pet shop. At the time, like most

people who buy puppies at a pet store, I had never heard of puppy mills and had no idea that my purchase might be contributing to animal cruelty. If I had, I would have explained to my kids that puppies sold in pet stores often come from greedy breeders who mistreat the dogs, keep them in filthy cages, and use them only to reproduce as quickly as possible. Then I would have gone to a shelter to adopt a dog.

By the time we adopted Lucy, we had been involved in animal rescue for many years. Lucy was a disaster of a dog when we got her. She had a bad case of kennel cough, and on the way home on the day we adopted her, I discovered she was in heat. It quickly became obvious that she had been abused, as she was terrified of people she didn't know, particularly men in baseball caps.

Shortly after we got her, Carl came in one day carrying a yardstick. Lucy whimpered, trembled, and hid under the bed. She did the same thing when she saw me with a flyswatter. Lucy weighs only ten pounds; it is incomprehensible to me that anyone would beat her, but that must be what had happened.

She was found running loose by an animal control officer in eastern Washington and was taken to a county shelter for strays. She was one year old. Because she was so fearful, the shelter staff felt she was not adoptable and turned her over to a rescue group that offered foster care. We got her from the rescue group.

It took a long time for Lucy to overcome her fears. She is ten now, and she is a silly, happy dog who gets so excited when she hears certain words, such as *walk* or *treat*, that she spins in circles. I say she "does doughnuts."

Lucy does doughnuts beside the door when I let her out, and she does doughnuts again on the other side when I let her back in. No matter which direction Lucy is headed, she's ecstatic about it. She jumps on my bed at night, waits while I brush my teeth, and then does doughnuts when I walk toward her. She likes to be groomed, but it's difficult to comb a dog who's spinning like a top.

*Me with Lucy*

Each morning when I say, "Let's go get the paper," Lucy acts as if she is the most fortunate dog ever born. Imagine being invited to walk down the driveway and back! What an opportunity! Lucky Lucy! She does doughnuts all the way to the door. Her enthusiasm is contagious, and never fails to make me laugh.

My driveway curves through the trees for the equivalent of a city block. On the return trip, Lucy always has tingly teeth. Because I'm carrying the newspaper, she wants to carry something, too. She often bit off pieces of fern or snatched a small pinecone. Then I began putting a small red ball in my pocket, to throw for Lucy.

She gets excited when she sees the ball and always chases it, but Lucy is not a retriever. She runs fast for about twenty feet, then drops the ball and waits for me to fetch it, and throw it again. If it bounces off the driveway into the bushes, it's *my* job to get it back, not hers.

One day I forgot to take the ball along. As I started back toward the house with my newspaper, Lucy danced in front of me, clearly waiting for me to fling the ball so she could run after it. I raised my arm high, "threw" an imaginary ball, and Lucy took off. She ran the usual twenty feet, then stopped and eagerly waited for me to "throw" the ball again. She seemed as happy with the pretend ball as she was when I threw the red one, and it's much easier for me to retrieve.

If Lucy were a person, she'd be a reader. When we read, especially fiction, we immerse ourselves in a pretend world that often seems as true and satisfying as our own lives. When I am writing a book, I think about my characters as if they were real people. I "see" them in my mind, and sense their feelings. I laugh at their jokes and cry over their sorrows. If they threw a ball, I would chase it.

No wonder I love my dog so much. We have a lot in common.

When we adopted Lucy, I believed we were rescuing her. In the end, she also rescued me by providing companionship and comfort after Carl died. When I come home, she is always overjoyed to see me, even if I've been gone only ten minutes. When I had pneumonia, she stretched out beside me on the bed, giving my hand occasional licks of encouragement. She is my loyal friend, always by my side.

Carl and I were both in our early sixties when we built the cabin. Some of our acquaintances were moving to retirement communities, and they questioned our decision to purchase country acreage at that time of our lives. Wouldn't it be more sensible, they asked, to buy a condo in town?

I have never regretted our choice. If we had not built

the cabin and created our sanctuary, I would not have viewed elk outside my windows, or watched the antics of band-tail pigeons, or seen newborn twin fawns. I would not have been here to rescue Buddy, or Mama and her kittens, or Gus, or any of the others. I would never have welcomed Mr. Stray into my life, or stood six inches from a black bear.

Something interesting is always happening here in the woods. This month, it's a raccoon who ate Mr. Stray's food and made a mess with his dirty paws in Mr. Stray's water bowl. I used the Iowa Children's Choice Award bell to chase him off the porch, and now I take the cat food and water in at night.

First a bear, and now a raccoon. When the Association of Iowa Media Educators gave me that bell, they didn't know how much I would use it—or for what purpose. Over the years, I've won four more Iowa Children's Choice Awards and received four more bells, but that first one is the biggest and works best for shooing bears and raccoons off my porch.

Curious to see what wildlife activity takes place at night, I purchased a trail camera. It is weatherproof, motion-activated, and takes either still photos or videos. My plan was to set it in a different spot each night, but so much happens on my front porch that most nights I leave it there.

The trail camera is my favorite toy. Some women

anticipate the next episode of their preferred soap opera. I wake up each morning eager to see video of what took place overnight on my porch. I have several fine close-ups of Mr. Stray's nose as he investigates the camera.

I quickly discovered why Mr. Stray's bowl is usually empty. He isn't the only one partaking of the cat buffet. The squirrels snatch pieces of dry cat food, as do the blue jays. The jays even eat canned tuna! Dillon, my neighbor Chris's cat, snacks frequently, as does Woody, a feral cat who was accidentally trapped when a neighbor was trying to relocate a 'possum. Because I'd had one hundred percent success taming stray cats and finding homes for them, I let the neighbor release Woody in my cat room.

Huge mistake! Woody climbed the walls, going up and down like a bungee jumper. Pictures crashed from the walls to the floor. Items on countertops scattered. Woody tore through the room like a wildcat, which is exactly what he was.

He eventually settled on top of the highest cupboard, coming down at night to eat. I know now that he should have gone straight to a spay-neuter clinic and then been released.

Woody spent six weeks in my cat room before I deemed him untamable. I couldn't catch him and when I brought the trap into the room, he stayed on his cupboard, not even coming down to eat. I had no choice but to turn him loose, but I felt terrible to let him go without having him neutered.

I worried that he would fight with Mr. Stray, but video shows the two of them together with no problem. Woody lives in the forest but is never seen in the daytime. If I didn't have the trail camera, I wouldn't know he's still here.

Then a new feral cat began hanging around. He, too, only came at night, loudly announcing his arrival by yowling. If I turned on the lights and looked out while he was there, he ran off. I called him Spook.

After he'd been here a few weeks, I decided to do the trap-neuter-return with him. I retrieved the trap from the attic, activated it on my porch, and draped a towel over the top.

When I looked out on the third morning, I could tell the trap contained a cat. Expecting Spook, I lifted the towel, and there sat Woody! I was up early that day, so I dressed quickly, loaded the trap in my car, and drove to a spay-neuter clinic that takes feral cats without an appointment. Woody got neutered and had a rabies shot. He stayed overnight at the clinic and then spent six more days back on top of the cupboard in the cat room, to be sure his incision was completely healed before I let him go.

As I opened the door for him, I felt lucky to have had a second chance with Woody. This time as I watched him leave,

I knew he would never be responsible for litters of unwanted kittens.

Meanwhile, I had continued to set the trap for the elusive Spook. The day after I released Woody, the trap got sprung in the middle of the day. When I lifted the towel and looked in the trap, Mr. Stray looked back! I would not have been more astonished if I'd found a baboon in that trap.

I put Mr. Stray in the cat room and began trying to tame him. Progress was slow. After two weeks, I still had not touched him, although he no longer hid when I entered the room.

I made an appointment with my vet to have Mr. Stray examined. Heidi helped me coax him into the carrier and Dr. Wood agreed to give him gas so that the exam wouldn't be so stressful for him. Once he was asleep, Dr. Wood invited me to come to watch.

My first question was, "Is this really Mr. Stray, or is it Ms. Stray?"

Her answer was a huge surprise. "It's definitely Mr. Stray," she said, "but he has already been neutered!"

I was temporarily speechless. Finally I said, "Then he must have been someone's pet."

She had already scanned him and found no microchip. "Perhaps someone did for him what you did for Woody," she said. "Maybe he was trapped, neutered, and released."

I nodded. That would explain his aversion to the trap during the first years he was here.

*Mr. Stray's new house*

The feral cat clinic that neutered Woody takes the tip off the left ear of each feral cat so that they can be released immediately if they're ever caught again. Mr. Stray's ear had not been tipped. Perhaps that practice was more recent.

Mr. Stray tested negative for HIV and feline leukemia. He did not have ear mites. He got a flea preventative. He was wormed, had his toenails clipped, and got vaccinated for rabies and distemper.

While all this was happening, Dr. Wood said it was okay for me to pet him. Happy tears pooled in my eyes as, at long last, I stroked Mr. Stray's soft fur.

When he awakened, I brought him home to the foster

cat room. He seemed glad to be in familiar surroundings, but when I checked on him an hour later, he hissed at me—the first hiss since I'd had him inside.

He never got any tamer. If anything, he withdrew more. He hid under a workbench or back in a corner all day, hissing if I came too close. I set up the camera in his room at night and watched as he batted a catnip mouse and a Ping-Pong ball around. He ate and used his litter box only at night.

I spent hours sitting in the cat room, reading, hoping he'd get used to my presence and move around while I was there, but he never did.

I loved knowing that Mr. Stray was safe, but I also knew that he had been happier when he was outside hunting mice and rolling on the brick path in the sun. Four weeks after his trip to the vet, I opened the door of the cat room and let Mr. Stray go out.

He didn't bolt as Woody had. He simply stepped calmly out the door and picked up his old life right where he had left off the day he got trapped. Now he's back on the porch, sleeping in his heated house, and waiting for me to bring his meals. We still have our conversations.

I believe I did the right thing in letting him free, but I hold close the memory of the day that I got to pet him. Because he was sedated, he didn't purr, but I hope he felt my loving hands anyway.

# I Wonder What's Next

At the end of a talk I gave recently at a children's literature festival in Warrensburg, Missouri, I took questions from the audience, most of whom were students in the ten-to-thirteen age range. One girl asked, "How old are you?"

Teachers usually roll their eyes at this question, but kids are often curious about my age, and I don't mind telling them the truth.

"I'm seventy-three years old," I said.

To my surprise, the audience began applauding! They clapped and cheered, and I had a hard time settling them down. I told them, "Don't cheer for my age; that isn't any accomplishment. I had no choice about growing old. The hard part was writing all of these books." Then they whooped some more.

Several years earlier, at a similar conference, a child had asked how long I'd been married. Carl was with me then, so I pointed him out to the audience and told them we'd been married for forty-five years. The kids whistled and hollered that time, too. Afterward, Carl insisted they were cheering him, for putting up with me all those years. He may have been right.

*Anne, holding her dog, Otter, and me with Lucy*

Readers sometimes ask how long I'll keep writing books. Most people my age have retired. Financially, I am able to retire. Physically, I really should retire. But mentally, emotionally, I am nowhere near ready to call it quits. Writing is not a typical job; it is a way of life. Writing a book is challenging and exhilarating. I like both the process and the results.

I believe that the work I do is important. When a parent or teacher tells me that, because of my books, a child has learned to love reading, I know I've made a positive difference that will last long into the future.

Helping animals is also a way of life. An animal rescue is not so much a one-time event as it is a mind-set, a willingness to get involved and to commit time, energy, and love to any needy creatures who happen to cross my path.

Through my books, I try to impart my belief in the sanctity of life. I hope to help readers expand their natural love for their own pampered puppy or cuddly kitten to include empathy for all living creatures.

Now that I travel less and no longer spend many weeks each year doing school visits, I lead a more literary life filled with books, study, and time to think. When I sit on my garden bench, watching the birds and making sure Lucy stays out of trouble, I am restored by my peaceful surroundings. I feel privileged to care gently for my small patch of Earth and the critters who share this space with me.

When we moved to the cabin, we hoped to spend at least ten years here. Carl got only five. I've now been here twelve years and plan to remain for the rest of my life. However long I'm here, the animals will always be welcome.

# Acknowledgments

Thanks to:

Buckley Veterinary Clinic for providing quality care for all of my rescued animals, as well as my own pets.

Rosanne Lauer, extraordinary editor, animal lover, and friend.

Ginger Knowlton of Curtis Brown, Ltd., who is efficient and supportive, and who writes e-mails that are always fun to read.

Anna Umansky for handling so many details with competence and good cheer.

Regina Castillo for copy-editing expertise, Irene Vandervoort for designing a perfect jacket, and all of the other talented folks at Dutton Children's Books. It is an honor to be a Dutton author.

Christine Pittman for caring as much as I do about all animals, and for helping me in numerous ways—including the delivery of fresh eggs from "the girls."

Vicki Taylor who photographed many cats for my rescue flyers, and always says yes when I need a favor.

Special thanks and huge hugs to everyone who adopted one of my rescued cats.